FOUNDERS OF THE WELFARE STATE

A series from NEW SOCIETY

edited by PAUL BARKER

Gower

First published 1984 by Heinemann Educational Books

Reprinted 1986 by
Gower Publishing Company Limited
Gower House
Croft Road
Aldershot
Hants GU11 3HR
England

British Library Cataloguing in Publication Data

Barker, Paul, *1935–*
    Founders of the welfare state.
    1. Social reformers—Great Britain—
    Biography
    I. Title
    362'.922   HN390

    ISBN 0-566-05295-4
    ISBN 0-566-05262-8 Pbk

Phototypesetting by The Castlefield Press, Moulton, Northants
Printed and bound in Great Britain by
Biddles Ltd, Guildford and King's Lynn

CONTENTS

362.922
B273

Preface		ix
TOWARDS THE WELFARE STATE	*Asa Briggs*	1
EDWIN CHADWICK	*Rudolf Klein*	8
JOSEPHINE BUTLER	*Pat Thane*	17
JOSEPH CHAMBERLAIN	*Denis Judd*	24
OCTAVIA HILL	*Peter Malpass*	31
CHARLES BOOTH	*Philip Waller*	37
EBENEZER HOWARD	*Peter Hall*	45
THE WEBBS	*Jose Harris*	52
R.L. MORANT	*Harry Judge*	61
LLOYD GEORGE	*John Grigg*	68
SEEBOHM ROWNTREE	*John Veit Wilson*	75
ELEANOR RATHBONE	*Jane Lewis*	83
WILLIAM BEVERIDGE	*Tony Lynes*	90
R.H. TAWNEY	*J.M. Winter*	98
ANEURIN BEVAN	*Kenneth O. Morgan*	105
RICHARD TITMUSS	*Jim Kincaid*	114
DRAWING CONCLUSIONS	*David Donnison*	121
Notes on Contributors and Further Reading		135

121, 347

History books begin and end, but the events they describe do not.

R.G. COLLINGWOOD, *An Autobiography*

PREFACE

I only ever met two of the people discussed in this book – R.H. Tawney and Richard Titmuss. Tawney I met when I was on one of my first jobs as a journalist. I had to report on a speech he was giving at the Working Men's College in Camden Town, for the *Times Educational Supplement*. This would be in 1959 or 1960. After it, I remember, he spent more time than he had any need to, talking to an inexperienced and, I am sure, rather brash reporter. He found out that I was from the West Riding, and he reminisced to me about Halifax, where he had taught WEA classes. I came away with the feeling I've retained ever since – that I had been lucky enough to be in the presence of a sort of secular saint. He emanated kindliness and goodness. I know I am not the only person who felt the same way.

Richard Titmuss I met when I was already Editor of New Society. He had always been rather wary of the magazine, or that was the impression I got – perhaps because it had been set up under non-socialist auspices. There was a big reception at the Banqueting Hall in Whitehall, to celebrate some anniversary of the official statistical services. The most famous ex-government statistician was the Prime Minister, Harold Wilson; he gave a witty speech. I ran into Titmuss enjoying a quiet cigarette at the back, and we went off for a meal together at Bianchi's in Soho. I liked him a lot. But I ended up with the strong impression that, alongside his highmindedness, Titmuss was very much an operator – a man who knew how to get what he wanted. Clearly, to be a successful reformer, you need something of both.

My observations of Tawney and Titmuss are personal. Some people would turn them around. They might describe Tawney, the ex-leader writer, as a bit of a windbag, and Titmuss as the secular saint. (Certainly the almost skeletal Titmuss had the more ascetic face for the part.) Whichever way you put it, the two men themselves felt they had a lot in common. When Tawney's *Equality* was reissued in paperback, Titmuss wrote a new introduction to it. I have it on my shelves now.

The present book is, of course, only one way to look at the history of the welfare state. It brings it down to biographies. You could turn this, too, the other way up and look only at broad themes. Many books have. Nonetheless, I hope that the essays collected here will be useful. They are not as separate as they might at first seem to be. There are many interlinkings.

The essays may seem to imply "progress," on an almost Victorian model, from the first glimmerings of something that might be called a welfare state to later, better years. But they also make it clear that it didn't always seem like progress at the time. Today many critics, of both left and right, will say you could write of the disasters of the welfare state, just as easily as of its successes. Its central achievements, such as the National Health Service, should not be underrated. But no social institution, including the welfare state, is ever complete: society is not a marble monument.

Apart from Asa Briggs's introduction and David Donnison's conclusion, which were specially commissioned for this book, all of these essays first appeared in the pages of New Society. The idea of a series like this was one which we'd turned over from time to time; it was precipitated into print by a suggestion from Peter Malpass. I am grateful to him for this; and I am grateful to Brian Abel-Smith, Nicholas Deakin, David Donnison, Roy Parker and Peter Townsend for helping me decide which of the founding mothers and fathers of the welfare state should go in. To Richard Bourne I owe a special debt because, without his help in commissioning the essays, the series could never have appeared when it did.

PAUL BARKER

TOWARDS THE WELFARE STATE

Asa Briggs

There was no one single impulse behind the making of the welfare state. Yet during the late 1940s it sometimes seemed as if there had been one. It was then that it was suggested, as part of a Whig-like interpretation, that history had culminated in the social legislation of the postwar Labour government. The term, *welfare state*, came into general use at this time, and a good deal of 19th century as well as 20th century history was re-written in the light of the achievements of social democracy. There was even a sense of finality – as there had been in the story of representative government – although Richard Titmuss and others were warning voices at the time, suggesting that there could be no finality in social processes. Instead, Richard Titmuss always put "welfare state" between inverted commas.

More convincing than the search for distant origins was the distinction sometimes drawn between, on the one hand, welfare and the complex network of social services which were introduced to enhance it or even to guarantee it, and on the other hand, the state and the wider powers conferred upon it as the social services were extended. Such a distinction had been drawn by Hubert Bland in one of the most interesting contributions to *Fabian Essays* in 1889: "it is not so much to the thing the state does as to the end for which it does it that we must look before we decide whether it is a socialist state or not." Already before 1914 there were critics of "collectivism" like the jurist, A.V. Dicey, who complained of the increase in the powers (and costs) of "the state" as new social services were introduced. But there were always counter-critics who switched the argument back to poverty, to social contingencies and social rights, and to what T.H. Marshall was to call during the late 1940s "citizenship and social class."

Although the 19th century saw a "growth in government," which is of increasing interest to social and economic as well as constitutional historians, there were, in fact, few people in Britain before 1914 who wished consciously to increase the powers of the state, and the few that there were could be accused of turning to German idealism (or practice) for their ideology. Voluntarism was an element in the British tradition, and the merits of self-help, including mutual self-help, were sung as loudly – or more loudly – in Scotland and in Wales as in England. Even the early Fabians directed attention to the role of the municipality and, in the case of the Webbs, to the role of the trade union. There were municipal socialists who were chary of state socialism, and trade unionists who preferred to attempt to secure social gains through their own struggles rather than through "reliance on the state."

Welfare objectives figured prominently on the agenda of trade union conferences, but the idea of continuous state intervention was not acceptable. As Henry Pelling has shown, the agents of the state were no more popular with the late 19th century working classes than the agents of Edwin Chadwick's public health policies had been popular with the mid-19th century middle classes. Indeed, they did not usually have behind them a moral force equivalent to the "sanitary idea" which, for all the talk of bullying a nation into health, won many middle class converts. There were similar working class doubts about education – about teachers as well as about attendance inspectors – although the situation was better in 1914 than it had been decades earlier. By 1909 one board school headmaster was writing with relief of improved relations between parents and teachers – "much more friendly: hostility, insolence, violence or threats, common in 1882, now hardly ever occur."

By then new routines were establishing themselves, and while the idea of creating a "welfare state" was still not a conscious objective of most reformers before 1914, the Liberal Lloyd George got near to envisaging it towards the end of the period, when he wrote in 1911 to his private secretary, R.G. Hawtrey, the remarkable lines quoted by John Grigg here in his account of Lloyd George's contribution to welfare state history:

"Insurance necessarily temporary expedient. At no distant date hope state will acknowledge full responsibility in the matter of making provision for sickness, breakdown and unemployment."

Lloyd George's insurance schemes in 1911 have often been seen as alternatives to the Webbsian philosophies of the Minority Report of the Royal Commission on the Poor Laws of 1909, and certainly they took the sting out of the Webbsian campaign. Yet Lloyd George deliberately saw insurance as a "temporary expedient," and in his 1909 budget speech had talked of making poverty as extinct as the wolves which had once wandered through the forests. Moreover, while the introduction of social insurance has been seen as a force delaying the break-up of the Poor Law, Lloyd George went on in the same note to predict that it would end in the abolition of the Poor Law.

The responsibility of the state had been demonstrated, he believed, in the 1834 Poor Law, but under conditions which had been so "harsh and humiliating that working class pride revolts against accepting so degrading and doubtful a boon." The stigmas were, in fact, incompatible with full citizenship. "Gradually," Lloyd George concluded, using a favourite Fabian adverb, "the obligation of the state to find labour or sustenance will be realised . . . Insurance will then be unnecessary." It is proper, therefore, as John Grigg explains, to see in this passage an anticipation of the "welfare state" which incidentally went further than any passage in the writings of his great contemporary and colleague, Winston Churchill, who had found a magic of his own in the notion of social insurance.

The chapters in this book deal with individual contributions to the making of the "welfare state" and they discuss, as they must, intentions as well as achievements, and the qualities of temperament and intellect which the successful struggle for welfare demanded. Yet the history of the making of the welfare state cannot be dealt with entirely in terms of individual contributions or the motivations that shaped them. Any satisfactory analysis of it must concern itself with economic and social forces, and with the variety of impulses which influenced the timing of legislation and the subsequent provision of resources. The scope and quality of administration must be studied within a changing economic, social – and political – context.

The first moves were made before the full development of the factory system, before the completed change to a predominantly urban society, before the reform of the civil service, before the advent of compulsory education, before the rise of the modern political party. And even in the early years of the 20th century, Lloyd George was more concerned with selling his land plan than with the massive problems of industrialisation.

The Benthamites at the beginning of the 19th century have often been compared with the Fabians at the end – both groups conscious of the need for a tabled agenda of government, both interested in the strategies of advance. Although in the debate about the Victorian state the crucial role of the Benthamites has been questioned, and in the debate about British socialism the role of the Fabians has been subjected to critical scrutiny, it is undeniable that groups as well as individuals figured prominently in the story. And there were religious as well as intellectual groups. "The sense of sin," wrote Samuel Barnett, "has been the starting point of progress." The Quakers brought to the story a sense of concern, the Evangelicals a sense of mission. The Charity Organisation Society, within and around which many of the crucial battles were fought, rightly figures as prominently in the story as the Poor Law itself. Founded in 1869, it sought to ensure that charity, still a major source of welfare funds, should not be distributed indiscriminately or without careful attention to family circumstances, and it objected to any softening of the 1834 Poor Law.

The history of the charities links 19th century history with the history of the centuries before it; and some of the pioneers of the social services – and each one had its own distinctive history – looked back to the pre-industrial era. It is difficult, however, to trace back the modes either of inquiry or of provision to a time before the great growth of population and the development of market-oriented industry. The statistical mode of investigation, and the formulation of "political economy," belong to the first phase of the story. So, too, do the sense of system, the great public inquiries, the blue books and the machinery of inspection. Yet there were at least three links with the past.

First, the idea of government protecting the weakest elements in society was still a potent idea on the eve of, and during the struggles around, the 1834 Poor Law, with the Bradford factory reformer, Richard Oastler, urging government to care for "the poor and needy, because they require the shelter of the constitution and the laws more than any other classes." Second, the idea of social rights carried through from the past could be further sharpened in diatribes against "political economy." Third, when the present was contrasted with the past, it was the disruptive influence of industrialisation which was often stressed. "There were periods in the past," wrote Oastler, "when the labourer's wages were protected by statute, and the common foods of the working people . . . were prohibited from being made articles of speculation. Care was then taken that the labourer's hope of reward should not be cut off by the inordinate desire for gain in the capitalists." Forty years later, Arnold Toynbee conceived of social services as redressing the imbalances of the industrial revolution: they represented an attempt to restore social objectives which had been abandoned during the early stages of industrialisation. It was in similar vein that the Minority Report of the Royal Commission on Labour in 1894 urged that it was "high time that the whole strength and influence of the collective organisation of the community should be deliberately, patiently and persistently used to raise the standard of life of its weaker and most oppressed members.

If those were the links, the breaks were obvious. The logic of the new Poor Law of 1834, closely related as it was to the development of political economy, involved trying to think and feel in a new way: charity was suspect as well as legislation. The disciplines of the factory, and the "problems" of the industrial town and city, stimulated new responses. There was a sense, indeed, of social imperatives. But there was a new sense also of what could *not* be done. The economist, Nassau

Senior, might maintain in 1847–48 that "it is the duty of a government to do whatever is conducive to the welfare of the government," but in face of social change he insisted that the limit to this duty was "power." The power of the laws of political economy was more significant than any limits set to the coercive power of the law. And the laws of political economy were the laws of the market, as stern as the laws of Moses. When socialists and Chartists were unwilling to accept the logic of the political economy of capitalist competition, they were forced to produce a political economy of their own.

In the light of market-oriented industry the development of the social services came to be seen as "intervention" or "regulation" – the application of organised state power to modify the play of market forces on the lives of individuals and their families and to mitigate the most disturbing features of industrialisation. And although unflinching believers in the Poor Law of 1834 might question the modification and the mitigation, and socialists might question the value of "palliatives," the modification and the mitigation became a necessary part of the process. So also did the uneasy interplay of investigative inquiry and militant protest. With the growth of political parties, plans for modification and mitigation could be written into authorised or unauthorised programmes.

If Bentham had envisaged Ministries of Education and Health, while stressing that in Britain "abundance of useful things are done by individuals which in other countries are done either by government or not at all," the Fabians in new political circumstances noted the pragmatic aspects of the record of intervention and regulation while stressing their commitment to socialism. In *Fabian Essays*, Sidney Webb summarised in characteristic language what had happened in the decades before 1889:

"In the teeth of the current political economy, and in spite of all the efforts of the mill-owning Liberals, England was compelled to put forth her hand to succour and protect her weaker members . . . Slice after slice has gradually been cut from the profits of capital, and thereby from its selling value, by strictly beneficial restrictions on the user's liberty to do what he likes with it . . . On every side he is being registered, inspected, controlled, and eventually superscaled by the community . . . All this has been done by 'practical men,' ignorant that is to say, of any scientific sociology, believing socialism to be the most foolish of dreams . . . Such is the irresistible sweep of social tendencies, that in their every act they worked out to bring about the very socialism they despised."

The vagueness of the key phrase, "the irresistible sweep of social tendencies," and the identification of what had happened through intervention before 1889 as "socialism," point to much in common with what Dicey had to say, although the conclusions of the Fabians were radically different.

Nonetheless, whatever either of them said it was not only "practical men" or "bureaucrats" who were responsible for changes in outlook, nor the "reformers" described and assessed in this book. Charles Dickens, vague or contradictory though he could be in his suggested "remedies" for social ills, exposed many of those ills and insisted on goodwill in a market society. Matthew Arnold pleaded for a very active governmental policy in education. George Eliot, like Charles Kingsley, extolled the "sanitary idea." John Ruskin, who urged that it was "the first duty of the state to see that every child born therein shall be well housed, clothed, fed and educated until it attains years of discretion," did not disguise his opinion that "the government must have an authority over the people of which we now do not so much as dream."

Such messages were not simply negative, particularly when they dwelt on the importance of education. Nor were they asking simply for "intervention." Despite increasing interest in the provision of the minimum during the late 19th century and the first years of the 20th, there was a strongly positive side to the argument. The individual was to be given a chance to realise his potential: society was to be liberated from the centuries-old tyranny of fate. Much of the moral force behind mid-20th century "welfare statism" had 19th century origins.

There was, of course, moral force also in the voluntarist tradition, which has left its own legacies to the 20th century – family care, case work, community action. When, as Pat Thane shows here, Josephine Butler described the home as "the nursery of all virtue, the fountain-head of all true affection and the main source of the strength of our nation," she was at the same time condemning the idealisation of home as the justification for conditions which prevented its realisation.

By 1914 there was one new entrant into the scene, however, not present in 1834 and only present then in a strictly limited role – the mass electorate, which even in 1914 did not include women and did not include all men. Edwin Chadwick, like Nassau Senior, feared the extension of the suffrage to the working classes. The "laws of political economy" would be subverted in the name of equality, and "the quest for popularity" would lead rich men to subvert the poor at election times by offering lavish promises." Chadwick lived long enough to read Joseph Chamberlain's famous question and answer in his ransom speech of 1885: "What ransom will property pay for the security it enjoys? . . . Society owes a compensation to the poorer classes of this country."

It would be a mistake to simplify 19th and 20th century history by condensing it in the form of the proposition that, once the battle for the vote had been won, the battle for what to do with it began, since what to do with the vote had been at issue long before the first battle was won – for example, throughout the Chartist agitation. Yet with the extension of the suffrage, new elements of political calculation were brought into the equation while new political pressures were generated. Lloyd George's statements belong to a new era, an era when Liberalism had already become torn with complex contradictions and when a new Labour Party, pledged to the use of political power, had been born. And before 1914 there were, as we can see in retrospect, obvious links with the future. The first career of William Beveridge, for example, had already led him into an examination of the welfare issues with which he will always be associated, though he never approved of the label, the "welfare state." Between then and now were two world wars, raising new expectations, and an unpredicted interwar depression, with all the mass unemployment that went with it; and it was out of that crucible of new experience that the welfare state was born.

EDWIN CHADWICK
1800–90

Rudolf Klein

If any warning against using stereotypes in analysing the development of social policy is needed, it is offered by the career of Sir Edwin Chadwick: the hero-villain of social reform in the first half of the 19th century. As the author of 1842 *Report on the Sanitary Condition of the Labour Population of Great Britain*, Chadwick secured a prominent place in the pantheon of social reform: the first of the great social engineers, who saw the transformation of the environment through state action as the key to both health and prosperity. As the main author of the 1834 *Poor Law Report*, however, Chadwick secured an equally prominent place in the gallery of social oppressors: the archetype of the ruthless ideologue who justified the horrors of the workhouse in the name of promoting individual responsibility.

Through the history books there still stalks the caricature Chadwick, the ruthless and heartless individualist: as in E.P. Thompson's *The Making of the English Working Class*. But among his contemporaries he was pilloried and abused because of his reforming zeal, inspired by – in the words of Sir John Simon, the great health reformer – his "indignation . . . at the spectacle of so much needless human suffering."

Chadwick's life almost spanned the 19th century. Born in 1800, he died in 1890. The son of a failed businessman turned successful journalist who was an admirer of Tom Paine and a life-long radical, Edwin was educated by his father and private tutors: a fact which reflected not the family's wealth but its position in the social fringe of the radical intellectuals.

If Chadwick was never accepted by the Whig or Tory political establishments, he was fully accepted by the intellectual establishment of philosophic radicals who dominated the world of ideas during the first half of the 19th century: the world of the political economists like James and John Stuart Mill, Ricardo and (Chadwick's special patron) Nassau Senior. Trained as a lawyer, Chadwick never practised (although he always tended to interrogate facts rather like a prosecuting barrister). Instead, he became a freelance journalist and, most important, Jeremy Bentham's assistant.

It was the influence of Bentham's system of ideas – in particular, his iconoclastic insistence on testing all legislation and all institutions against the "greatest happiness" principle – which, together with the principles of the classical economists, shaped Chadwick's approach to social reform throughout his life. It was an approach which stressed that policy should be determined by the application of clear-cut principles, not by the operations of special interest groups. It saw individual self-interest as the mainspring of social action, while yet recognising the state's role in creating the legislative and institutional framework required if individual self-interest were to work to the benefit of society as a whole. (The doctrine of pure laissez-faire, as Lionel Robbins pointed out a long time ago, is not to be found in the writings of the classical utilitarians and economists and is largely the retrospective creation of Dicey in his attempt to show that the drift towards collectivism represented a betrayal of the principles of the founding fathers.)

On Bentham's death in 1832, Chadwick became a member of that curious and influential band of philosophic radicals who combined involvement in public administration, journalistic polemics and academic inquiry: a freedom which, eventually, was to be circumscribed by their own success in creating a professional bureaucracy and so drawing a demarcation line between administration and politics. For Chadwick, as for Mill, Macaulay and others, there was nothing inconsistent in holding administrative offices and engaging in the mobilisation of public opinion in support of their views. No pressure group – not even the Child Poverty Action Group – has ever been more assiduous in using the media and its network of contacts to promote its ideas.

First drawn into public administration as an investigator for the Royal Commission of Inquiry into the Poor Law in 1832, Chadwick was to become the main drafter of its report and then secretary of the commission set up to administer the new legislation. Subsequently, in 1848, he became a member of yet another Victorian quango – the General Board of Health – until he was hounded out of office in the mid-1850s. This marked the effective end of his career as a public servant although, until the end of his life, he remained active as an indefatigable pamphleteer and speaker at such bodies as the National Association for the Promotion of Social Science or the British Association for the Advancement of Science.

In the course of his career in public administration, Chadwick was also at various times involved in the framing of factory legislation and the reform of the police. But it is his part in the reform of the Poor Law and in the sanitary revolution that represents his major contributions to the shaping of social policy, and which best demonstrates the futility of trying to capture the nature of his role (and that of philosophic radicalism) in terms of simple stereotypes.

The pressures which led to the appointment of the Poor Law Commission, and the subsequent legislation implementing its recommendations, were long-standing, multiple and varied. There was the concern about the cost of support for the poor. There was the worry that outdoor relief – and especially the Speenhamland system, an early version of the Family Income Supplement, which subsidised the working poor – was undermining labour discipline. There was the Malthusian argument that subsidising the poor would only encourage them to breed, and thus accelerate the trend towards increasing "immiseration." This view led to the conclusion that there should be no support whatsoever for the pauper population (a view which was finally to triumph in article twelve of the Soviet constitution of 1936, which enunciated the principle that "he who does not work, neither shall he eat").

In short, the pressures driving the campaign for reform had little to do with Benthamism or philosophic radicalism, but largely reflected the desire of the landed classes to re-assert social control over "an increasingly numerous, truculent, and workshy peasantry who sent poor rates spiralling at a time of agricultural depression," to quote Anthony Brundage's analysis of the making of the New Poor Law.

However, the way in which the problem of pauperism was re-defined in the 1834 report, and the subsequent legislation, did reflect the influence of Benthamite principles as transmitted through Chadwick who, while no great intellectual innovator, had a rare gift for synthesising and systematising the ideas of others. Crucially, Chadwick rejected Malthusian pessimism, and with it the argument for ending all support for paupers. The real evil, as he saw it, of the existing Poor Laws was not that they encouraged the growth of population, but that they undermined incentives to work. If only the pauper could be forced back into the labour market – instead of being attracted from it by the allowance system – the problem would be solved.

From this definition of the problem, the solutions followed almost automatically. If the real problem stemmed from the system of allowances, then the solution was to abolish all forms of outdoor relief: to concentrate all support in the workhouse. If the real need was to force paupers into the labour market, and by so doing give them an incentive to seek work instead of relief, then it was essential to set support at a level below that which anyone could hope to earn in employment.

The logic of this solution led directly to the workhouse test and to the principle of "less eligibility" – the twin pillars of the New Poor Law. In future, there was to be only one test of need: whether the able-bodied pauper was prepared to enter a workhouse. This would be a "self-acting test of the claim of the applicant," in the words of the 1834 report.

Those administering the Poor Law would no longer have to distinguish "the really destitute from the crowd of indolent imposters." Relief would be automatic: "the able-bodied claimant should be entitled to immediate relief on the terms prescribed, wherever he might happen to be; and should be received without objection or inquiry; the fact of his compliance with the prescribed discipline constituting his title to a sufficient, though simple diet." This would get rid, at a stroke, of the "cumbrous and expensive barriers of investigations and appeals" in a discretionary system.

But, of course, the new system of automatic entitlement to relief could only work if it also reflected the principle of "less eligibility" – adapted by Chadwick from Bentham's *Panopticon*, the latter's vision of an ideal prison (an ominous and significant way of perceiving the role of the workhouse). "Every penny bestowed that tends to render the condition of the pauper more eligible than that of the independent labourer is a bounty on indolence and vice," the 1834 report argued. It was therefore essential that conditions in the workhouse should be less attractive – less eligible – than "the situation of the independent labourer of the lowest class." Only thus could paupers be encouraged to de-pauperise themselves: only thus could the right to relief be reconciled with the need to maintain the incentives and discipline of the labour market. The principles of the New Poor Law can thus be seen as an attempt to combine the requirements of all industrialising societies (whether capitalist or not) for labour discipline with the acceptance of collective responsibility for maintaining standards of subsistence for the whole population. The 1834 report was emphatic that its aim was not to deal with poverty, which it regarded as inevitable, but simply to prevent indigence – ie, starvation.

The new system led not only to literary denunciations from writers like Carlyle but also to political protest and riots. These were the natural reactions to what, in practice, often turned out to be a ruthlessly mean and dehumanising system. So it is not surprising that Chadwick himself came to be portrayed as a dogmatic, insensitive ideologue who created a machine for crushing people in the new bastiles. But it is important to analyse in some detail just why the New Poor Law turned out to be such a disaster. For only so can we solve the puzzle of why Chadwick – the dedicated enemy of "needless human suffering" – came to be associated with a reform which systematically generated humiliation: why a reform which introduced the principle that society should "ensure every individual belonging to it against the extreme of want," in John Stuart Mill's words, came to be perceived as an example of social tyranny.

One answer is that there was a fundamental flaw in Chadwick's analysis of the problem: a flaw which stemmed from the assumptions of the classical economists. Like Mrs Thatcher, they believed unemployment to be largely, if not wholly, self-induced. If the individual worker did not have a job, he had only himself to blame: it was either because he was indolent or because he was pricing himself out of the labour market (which is why the Speenhamland system was denounced with such fervour; it was seen as distorting the natural operations of the labour market).

But this is only part of the explanation. The New Poor Law not only represented the introduction of new principles in social policy. It also represented an attempt at an administrative revolution. It created, for the first time, a national body – the Poor Law Commission – in an attempt to enforce national standards. Parishes were to be amalgamated to form effective units of administration, where "efficient permanent officers" would be in charge. "We deem uniformity essential," the 1834 report argued, while recognising it might take time to achieve.

In the event, Chadwick – like so many social reformers since – found that his intentions were betrayed in their implementation. In a paper read to the Social Science Congress at Edinburgh in 1863, he reflected – with the benefit of hindsight – on the failure of the New Poor Law to achieve its full aims. Basically, he argued, the intentions of the reformers had been defeated by the power of local lobbies: the "sinister interests which operate most powerfully in narrow areas."

"Farmer guardians," he pointed out, "could still give, though indirectly, outdoor relief, which in effect was frequently relief in aid of the wages of their own employees . . . The owners of small tenements in towns could still, as guardians, give outdoor partial relief, much of which was in payment of high rents paid by their own tenants."

Here is the voice of the true radical reformer. Like so many social engineers, Chadwick was convinced that if only his ideas had been carried out ruthlessly and comprehensively enough, they would have succeeded. Once Chadwick had made up his mind – once his ideas were developed into a full-blown system where abstract principles were translated into a precise administrative machinery – nothing would shift him.

Indeed it is this which, perhaps, helps to explain his failure as an administrator. His career as secretary to the Poor Law Commission, from 1834 to 1842, was marked by a series of increasingly bitter and public rows with the commissioners, who finally relegated their domineering servant to an administrative limbo, virtually ignoring his existence. As Sir John Simon wrote, Chadwick lacked the quality of "judicial patience": he did not recognise sufficiently that social reform had to be based on the mobilisation of consent.

Simon was writing here about Chadwick in his role as the prophet of the sanitary revolution. But Chadwick's contribution in this role was remarkably similar to the part he played in the creation of the New Poor Law. Once again, he launched a crusade with a report – the 1842 *Report on the Sanitary Condition of the Labouring Population of Great Britain* – published in a large edition with carefully orchestrated publicity. Again, he succeeded in having legislation, based on his report's principles, enacted – if only in a watered-down version. Again, however, he stumbled when it came to implementing the legislation: the General Board of Health failed to overcome local resistance to its policies, and Chadwick himself became the main victim of this failure.

In turning his attention to sanitary reform, almost as a form of occupational therapy for his frustrations at the Poor Law Commission, Chadwick's starting point was the financial burden of disease on the poor rates. But the scope of his inquiry soon widened out. The outcome was a magisterial, comprehensive and horrendous indictment of social conditions in Britain, which makes chilling reading even today.

In the event, the ideas underlying the *Sanitary Report* were very different from those that had shaped the *Poor Law Report*. In it, Chadwick embraced wholeheartedly the environmental theory of disease prevention, brushing aside the claims of curative medicine. It was squalor, dirt and – above all – excrement which caused disease: "All smell is, if it be intense, immediate acute disease," he wrote. The so-called miasmatic theory of disease was soon to be discredited, but Chadwick's recipe for action was not: a good example of how bad theories can actually lead to successful social policies. Further, Chadwick concluded that it was poor social conditions, rather than indolence or lack of moral fibre, which caused poverty. Disease caused destitution; destitution did not cause disease.

In this emphasis on the crucial importance of transforming the environment in order to transform individual lives lay the key to social policy progress for the rest of the 19th century, and beyond. For if Chadwick's particular concern was with drainage and sewerage, precisely the same logic applied to improving housing and working conditions. In this lay the most enduring contribution of the *Sanitary Report*.

Equally important was the way in which Chadwick reached this conclusion: the methodology of analysis which shaped his report, and which has continued to influence social policy ever since. Page after page of the report is devoted to analysing variations in life expectancy by social class and place of residence, in an endeavour to identify the causes of disease. In Manchester, for example, the average age of death of "professional persons and gentry, and their families" was 38, while that of "mechanics, labourers, and their families" was 17; in rural Rutlandshire the equivalent figures were respectively 52 and 38. In this respect, the analysis was not so very different from that of the Black report, published in 1980.

In the event, the sanitary revolution turned out to be a long-drawn-out war of attrition with local vestries and local water companies, of which Chadwick was the first casualty. But although then effectively barred from active administration and politics – his attempts to become an MP failed abysmally – Chadwick continued the battle with words for another 35 years.

In a sense, most of his addresses and articles are a prolonged, and sometimes crotchety, self-justification. He adopted new enthusiasms, such as educational reform, but essentially his aim was to defend his two great reforms: the New Poor Law and the sanitary revolution. However, it is his language of justification which gives these later writings their fascination. For in them, he developed what was largely to be the language of social policy analysis for the next 100 years: asserting the claim of dispassionate reason – of scientific methods and bureaucratic rationality – as against the power of vested interests: the "baleful money interests" represented in parliament and the "jobocracies" of public companies, as well as the "imbecility, or the sinister interests of ignorant local administrators."

Facts and figures, as always, continued to be Chadwick's main weapon. Already in the *Sanitary Report*, he had begun to develop a cost-benefit approach to the analysis of social problems. Preventive measures, he had argued with a wealth of statistical evidence, could pay for themselves. It was a point to which he returned, again and again. "When the sentimentalist and the moralist fails, he will have as a last resource to call in the aid of the economist, who has in some instances proved the power of his art to draw iron tears from the cheeks of a city Plutus," he told the British Association in his presidential address in 1862.

Not only was waste sinful, but waste itself could become the source of sin: "it is my deep conviction that whilst waste is sinful, sin by the infliction of animal and human suffering is wasteful," Chadwick wrote (in an essay devoted to the regulation of the cab trade). People represented capital investment – he argued, in an early version of human capital theory – and maximising their welfare would also maximise national wealth. Poor social conditions not only lowered the productivity of labour but also generated social problems: "insanitary conditions are attended with moral as well as physical deterioration; crime following most closely those conditions where there is a perception of the short duration of life, and where the appetites for immediate enjoyment amongst the ill-educated and ill-trained are strong and reckless" – a contention backed up by a statistical table showing the relationship between crime rates and health indicators. In sharp contrast to the assumptions which had shaped the New Poor Law, Chadwick had come to see the poor as the victims of their circumstances: a conclusion which demanded collective social action rather than individual moral rehabilitation.

One of Chadwick's main concerns, therefore, remained the principles and practice of social regulation. "It will not do, however, to base legislation on beneficence, or on the heroic virtues, and the great problem is to unite interest with duty," he stressed. The challenge was to create a framework of state regulation and intervention which would give individuals incentives to behave in the public interest. It was a principle which led him to advocate more and more intervention: in particular, public control of water authorities and railways. Unregulated competiton between small firms – whether for the cab horse trade or for funerals – was inefficient: far better have one, publicly regulated, monopoly enterprise (a long cry, this, from the classical free market doctrine).

In turn, this required improved methods of legislation and more professional administration. Chadwick's contempt for democratic politics – whether national or local – grew with age. Instead of starting with an inquiry into facts, legislation reflected the prejudices of public men. Instead of the "close and secret" cabinet procedure for preparing legislation, there should be open inquiries: "In legislation, as in other things, gross ignorance sees no difficulties, imperfect knowledge descries them, perfect knowledge overcomes them." In local government, matters were worse still, since it was the self-interested who had the greatest incentive to participate, with the result that "the performance of honorary municipal duties, instead of devolving upon the highest class of citizens, is sinking into the hands of the lowest grade of persons of the middle classes." From this followed the need for a more professionalised bureaucracy.

In all this, Chadwick anticipated most of the themes that were to occupy social reformers for the next century. He was a pioneer not only in developing methods of social inquiry for analysing problems but also in realising that devising solutions meant designing new instruments of administration. Like so many social reformers since, he was a man dominated by a "strain after perfection which necessarily becomes one-sided in a world of many mixed considerations," in the words of one politician sympathetic to him. This "strain after perfection" helps to explain both his immediate failure to achieve his aims and his long-term influence. An opinionated optimist, sustained by his conviction that social engineering exploiting the knowledge of the social sciences could transform the world, Chadwick may often seem naive and over-simple in the present age of disillusion and pessimism. But it is difficult not to be impressed by his intrepid, single-minded conviction that rational analysis could defeat the forces of ignorance, prejudice and self-interest, and create a better society.

JOSEPHINE BUTLER
1828–1906

Pat Thane

Josephine Butler is not an immediately obvious candidate for the ranks of pioneers of the welfare state. She is best remembered as a leading campaigner against the Contagious Diseases Acts of the 1860s, which attempted to regulate prostitution in Britain – a sphere of activity not normally within even the more elastic definitions of state welfare. However, her concern with prostitution derived from, and remained indissolubly linked with, a passionate hostility to social injustice – especially where women were its victims – which drew her into a wider range of philanthropic activities.

On this basis, she merits a place in this book in her own right. But she is also a representative of the many impressive women of the 19th century whose devotion to philanthropy is too easily sneered at. They not only brought real relief to intolerable lives, but sustained a struggle against inequality which underpinned much subsequent state action.

Josephine Butler's background could stand as surrogate for that of many such women. She was born in 1828, the seventh child of John and Hannah Grey of Dilston, Northumberland. She was related to the ruling Whig aristocracy. Lord Grey, the Whig Prime Minister during the struggle over the 1832, Reform Act was her father's cousin. But she identified with, and quintessentially belonged to, the provincial, radical, professional, evangelical middle class – the historically unique social group which gave birth to most of the distinguished philanthropists and reformers of the 19th century. They were the products and beneficiaries of a new industrial society, but they were also, and crucially, its socially acceptable critics. They stood outside direct involvement in industry or politics, and were the conscience which pricked at society's harder, more exploitative instincts, without threatening to undermine it.

Josephine Butler's father was an agricultural reformer and anti-slavery campaigner, from whom she learned a real hatred of injustice, a "horror of slavery and all arbitrary power," and the necessity for active commitment to achieve change. Like many other females later active in feminist and reforming campaigns, she was not educated, as the stereotype would have it, for a life of leisured domesticity. Her father encouraged her to acquaint herself with social and political questions and in her early adolescence read with her the government blue books and exposés of social conditions. From her mother, a Moravian, Butler acquired a deep commitment to Evangelical Christianity. In late adolescence – like other contemporary philanthropists – she experienced a religious crisis which strengthened her commitment. She saw no conflict between her father's social and political radicalism and her mother's Christianity. Indeed, she regarded them as perfectly complementary. "I never understood," she later wrote, "saving souls only. I understood better saving a whole man or woman, both soul and body."

An important influence on her early life was her aunt, Margaretta Grey, a strong-minded feminist who "was so disgusted at finding she was not allowed to enter parliament when her cousin was leader of the Whigs . . . that she made it a custom to obtain admission by dressing as a boy." Josephine also had close links with European republican circles through her father and other relatives. She was a frequent visitor to Europe, a good linguist, and a close observer of the political upheavals of the mid-19th century.

In 1851, she married George Butler, an Anglican clergyman and subsequently an examiner to Oxford University, vice-principal of Cheltenham College and principal of Liverpool College, who shared her religious, social and political beliefs. They had four children. The marriage was, and remained, profoundly happy. George encouraged Josephine's public life, experiencing setbacks in his own career because of her notoriety.

In the first years of their marriage she devoted herself to home-making but, not surprisingly given her background, grew angry with the social and intellectual conservatism of male-dominated Oxford society. She was furiously frustrated by the stolid refusal of Oxford men to treat seriously the views of even so intelligent and well-informed a woman as herself. After five years she escaped to Cheltenham, on doctors' advice, following a respiratory illness. This was the first of a series of physical and nervous breakdowns which recurred throughout her life (as in those of so many prominent 19th century figures), especially when she was under-occupied. They did not prevent her remaining actively alive to the age of 78.

Her four children were born in Cheltenham and one, Eva, her only daughter, died suddenly and tragically. The Butlers moved almost immediately to Liverpool where Josephine, aged 36, "became possessed with an irresistible urge to go forth and find some pain keener than my own, to meet with people more unhappy than myself." In the misery of Liverpool in the 1860s this was not difficult, and she began to translate her commitments into action.

She began by visiting women picking oakum in the vast Liverpool workhouse. Attractive, always fashionably and prettily dressed, genuinely unpatronising in her speech and attitude, she won real trust from the women, and others came to her for help. But she increasingly felt that it was the prostitutes who needed her most. There were hundreds of them in a poor port city, with few places of refuge. Josephine took those whom she could into her house. She was incensed by the contempt of other male and female philanthropists for women whom she saw as victims of poverty and injustice, rather than of sin. She identified as the cause of their poverty the effect of industrialism – even more than previous economic systems – in providing more and better-paid jobs for men than for women.

"Women," she wrote, "have unequal access to work and to self-support at a time when increasing numbers need it." The popular justification for this inequality she rightly identified as "the constantly reiterated assertion that 'woman's sphere is in the home'." She went on: "The saying, as it is uttered now, in the face of the great facts of society as they lie confessed before us, is to a large extent wholly inapplicable, and assumes the character of a most ungentle irony . . . Yet there remain both men and women who continue solemnly to inform the women who are striving for some work or calling, which will save them from starvation and who have no human being but themselves to depend on, that their proper sphere is the home – that their proper function is to be wives and mothers and their happiness is to be dependent on men! . . . Like Pharaoh who commanded the Israelites to make bricks without the material to make them of, these moralisers command this multitude of inquiring women back to homes which are not and which they have not the material to create."

Not that she was hostile to the value of a happy home and family, such as she had herself always experienced, and had been supported and loved by. "I believe," she wrote in the same volume, "that the Home is the nursery of all virtue, the fountainhead of all true affection and the main source of the strength of our nation." But she revolted passionately against the idealisation of home as the justification for conditions which prevented its realisation.

Fear of the disruption of the idealised home, she believed, lay at the root of much male opposition to female equality. Yet, she argued from experience, the happiest home was one in which males and females were equal in status and respect. Such happiness was only possible for the poor when they had material security which was, in turn, only attainable by them when women could earn equally with men. This was important for families headed by low-paid men, and still more so for the large number of female-headed households, resulting from widowhood, illness, and the inability of some women to marry in a society in which they outnumbered men.

Josephine Butler was convinced that it was the inability of women to earn an adequate wage by other means which drove them to prostitution. She felt equally passionately that this form of earning was only possible because of the prevailing double standard, which regarded sexual activity as normal for men but degrading for women. Hence respectable society unforgiveably divided women into two equally unrealistic groups: chaste madonnas on their pedestals, polluted magdalens in the gutter. And then had the effrontery to reject one of its own creations. This was, she insisted, not only unjust but un-Christian. Had not Christ himself shown as much care for the one group as for the other? Her experience had taught her that the poor, including prostitutes, were not more depraved than the rich, nor did they deserve inferior treatment.

Josephine Butler did not, as she justly condemned other philanthropists for doing, "go in" for prostitution as a good cause, dissociated from any understanding of the social and economic structures which produced that "cause." Admittedly, she did not consider whether equal access to the labour market for men and women might not create new problems when that market was already overstocked. But few to the right of the socialists confronted that, and she never pretended to toy with socialism.

From the late 1860s, then, her central commitment was to equal opportunities and status for men and women – social, economic and political. She believed that this in no way conflicted with the realisation of happy home lives, or with a version of the contemporary doctrine of "separate spheres." She thought that women had an especial instinct to care for others, and to create home-like environments in the worst conditions. She thought they would use political rights differently from men, to create a more just world: a view which, rightly or wrongly, feminists have not abandoned. That women should vote she believed was, simply, right. The absurdity of their exclusion she summed up towards the end of her life with the comment: 'Fancy *me* not having the vote!''

Although she felt that the poorest women needed her most, she was persuaded in 1867 to become president of the newly-formed Council for Promoting the Higher Education of Women. Its task was to create in the north institutions similar to those which had developed in the south since the foundation of Bedford College, London. The council was successful in providing university-level lectures for women which were the forerunners of the university extension movement; in pressing Cambridge University to provide exams for women; and in acquiring endowments for female institutions. Josephine Butler was as concerned for middle class as for working class women to acquire independence through the labour market. Higher education was the route to higher-status occupations.

But when, in 1869, parliament passed a third Contagious Diseases Act in a decade, she returned to the problem of prostitution. She agreed, with some timidity, and on the advice of Mazzini, to lead the campaign for the acts' repeal.

The Contagious Diseases Acts of 1864, 1866 and 1869 operated in 18 garrison towns and ports. They were introduced as exceptional legislation to combat the spread of VD among enlisted men. The chosen method consisted of the identification and registration of women as "common prostitutes" by plainclothes policemen. The women had then to undergo fortnightly internal examinations. If found to be suffering from gonorrhoea or syphilis, they were interned in a certified locked hospital for a period not to exceed nine months. A woman who resisted any stage of this process had the difficult task of proving her virtue before a magistrate.

Organised protest against the acts began in 1869, in response to efforts to extend the acts to the north. It was led by an at first entirely male National Association, which was soon joined by a parallel but separate and more energetic Ladies' National Association, led by Josephine Butler. This denounced the acts for their support of the double standard, and for their severe infringement of the civil rights of poor women. The acts did not attempt to restrain male use of prostitutes; to detect or treat male carriers of VD; or to help the women other than by treating their diseases. They imposed on women potential abuse and exploitation by police and doctors.

The campaign was carried on by a strong supporting network of women of similar backgrounds to Josephine Butler, as were so many of the women's movements of the later 19th century. They saw the campaign as one of women for women. Butler tried hard, with some success, to gather the active support of working class women, and also won over a number of men of all classes. She and her immediate colleagues acted with a courage which again belies the stereotype of the helpless Victorian female. To speak in public about sex was difficult and the response repellent, especially from some middle class men. They were impelled by religious, feminist and humane commitment. By 1883 they succeeded in convincing parliament that the legislation conflicted too crudely with official morality by sanctioning the existence of prostitution. The acts were repealed.

But the terms on which the campaign had had to be waged to achieve this effect – the upholding of a puritanical morality – was not entirely to Josephine Butler's liking, or an unmixed blessing in the outcome. The campaign brought little change in attitudes towards prostitutes; indeed, it did something to harden them. Many male and female campaigners devoted their energies after repeal to a Whitehouse-style campaign for "social purity," which led to the creation of local vigilante patrols, tracking down not only suspected prostitutes but also any young people thought to be seeking sexual pleasure. They carried out attacks on any social gatherings deemed to be potential sources of licentiousness.

Butler collaborated with this movement to the extent of campaigning with W.T. Stead for the Criminal Law Amendment Act, 1885, which raised the age of consent for females from 13 to 16, following Stead's exposé of child prostitution. Thereafter, she publicly dissociated herself from the narrower-minded excesses of "social purity." She felt that the movement reinforced the false emphasis on the sin and personal worthlessness of the poor, and diverted attention from the poverty which she believed was the cause of their apparent immorality.

The contagious diseases campaign had strengthened her original convictions. It increased her awareness of the working, living and health conditions of poor women; of the public and philanthropic institutions, which provided for them (or more often did not); and of the fragility of civil freedom in modern society. For the remainder of her life she campaigned on all of these issues. Her pamphlet, *Government by Police*, published in 1879, opened: "It seems probable that one of the greatest questions of the future will be that of ascertaining the best means of effectually counteracting or holding in check the strongly bureaucratic tendencies which we see to be stealing over almost every civilised nation."

As well as working for votes for women (she died in 1906, before the onset of militant suffragism), she campaigned against factory legislation, which restricted female hours of work and therefore the range of occupations open to them; against the Boers in the Boer war, an unusual stance for a radical Liberal, taken on the then unusual grounds that the Boers' treatment of the blacks rendered it irresponsible for Britain to give them a free hand in South Africa; in defence of Dreyfus; and for more humane welfare institutions.

Even in 1869 she shared the "pretty general realisation of the harm done by the old-fashioned Lady Bountiful way of dispensing alms and patronage." But she equally criticised the "tendency at present . . . to centralisation of rule, to vast combinations, large institutions and uniformity of system. I have a doubt about any wholesale manipulation of the poor, the criminal, scholars in school, etcetera. I believe it to be so far from founded on a philosophical view of human nature and of society that, if carried to extremes, the last state of our poor will be worse than the first . . . Nothing whatever will avail but the large infusion of Home elements into workhouses, hospitals, schools, orphanages, lunatic asylums, reformatories and even prisons . . . Everything lives and thrives best where there is the principle of play or freedom which home affords."

Her criticism was directed at the "uniformity of the system," advocated by the newly founded Charity Organisation Society, and its close ally, the Poor Law. She might have been equally uneasy about many of the institutions of the welfare state which have since emerged, and certainly about the infringements of civil liberties which have accompanied them. Like her diagnosis of the wrongs of women, inside welfare institutions and out, her fears of a century ago have a contemporary resonance.

Josephine Butler's contribution to the emergence of a welfare state of which she would not wholly have approved, nor entirely disapproved, was this. With a notable articulateness, she kept alive the pitifully unequal struggle against the uglier face of emerging industrial capitalism and institutionalised male domination. She spoke for a powerful sense of social justice and of the equal worth of people. And she expressed resistance to repression, exploitation and narrow-minded selfishness. Without such resistance, the good in the welfare state could not have been attained.

JOSEPH CHAMBERLAIN
1836–1914

Denis Judd

Joseph Chamberlain's career, viewed superficially, seems to allow him little or no claim to be considered a founder of the British welfare state. He occupied no ministerial position in either Liberal or Unionist governments that would have given him responsibility for introducing national welfare schemes, even if the times had been ripe for such innovations. In fact, during nearly 40 years in parliament, he held only three cabinet posts, those of President of the Board of Trade from 1880 to 1885, President of the Local Government Board, briefly, in 1886, and the Colonial Secretaryship from 1895 to 1903. Nor were the governments to which he belonged dedicated to vast schemes of social reform. During the 1880s, Gladstone became increasingly obsessed with solving the Irish problem, and from 1895 to 1903 Chamberlain was a Liberal Unionist member of a cabinet dominated by Conservatives and dependent on a Tory majority in the Commons.

Yet Chamberlain's impact upon contemporary Britain was out of all proportion to his ministerial career, with its early pitiful legislative achievements and its later, lopsided colonial emphasis. Above all, Chamberlain was a man convinced of the wisdom of his view of things, and he never ceased to promote public discussion of the great issues of his times. His creative intelligence, and his capacity for rational analysis, were enhanced by quite extraordinary powers of exposition – including a demagoguery which enabled him to draw huge crowds to his public meetings and to hold his audiences spellbound. Chamberlain's crowd-pulling style is nicely illustrated by a conversation overheard between two Bristol men during his great tariff reform campaign of 1903–06:

FIRST MAN: I'm a poor man and I can't afford to pay ten shillings for a seat in the gallery.

SECOND MAN: It's worth paying a guinea just to see him say "Free Fooder."

Chamberlain's social origins put him unequivocally on the side of reform during the most formative years of his life. The eldest son of a convinced Unitarian, he belonged to a Dissenting tradition that led him naturally into Liberal politics by way of a brilliantly successful, and profitable, career as a Birmingham manufacturer.

Chamberlain's commitment to active radical politics was confirmed during the mass agitations for an extension of the parliamentary franchise between 1858 and 1866, and he later recalled those "great meetings . . . The men poured into the hall, black as they were from the factories . . . The seats then used to be removed from the body of the hall, and the people were packed together like herrings." Chamberlain soon set about organising the herrings, and became a leader of the Birmingham Liberal Association which, after the Reform Act, 1867, ensured that the local Liberal vote should be so marshalled as to elect the party's candidates to the city's three parliamentary seats.

In 1873, Chamberlain became Lord Mayor of Birmingham after a crushing defeat of the Tories in the municipal elections. For over three years he supervised a hectic programme of civic change that established his reputation as an advanced social reformer. Although it has been argued that his slum clearance schemes were largely cosmetic, Chamberlain forced through a variety of measures that can only be described as municipal socialism. Birmingham corporation bought out the private gas and water companies, thus making these two essentials both cheaper and subject to democratic control. Chamberlain flung public and private funds behind a systematic programme of municipal improvement over and above his assualt on contaminated water, inadequate sewers, badly paved and unlit streets, and slum tenements. The central and branch libraries, the art gallery, and various collections, were enlarged and enriched. Municipal swimming baths, new parks and public gardens were opened. Many new schools were built.

As significant as these achievements was the style in which Chamberlain justified them. Speaking in October 1874 in Birmingham, he struck out at the root cause of Britain's social problems:

"I am a radical reformer because I would reform and remove ignorance, poverty, intemperance, and crime at their very roots. What is the cause of all this ignorance and vice? Many people say that intemperance is at the bottom of everything, and I am not inclined to disagree with them. I believe we hardly ever find misery or poverty without finding that intemperance is one of the factors in such conditions. But at the same time I believe intemperance itself is only an effect produced by causes that lie deeper still. I should say these causes, in the first place, are the gross ignorance of the masses; and, in the second place, the horrible, shameful homes in which many of the poor are forced to live."

A year later, he introduced his massive scheme for slum clearance.

These three years of whirlwind activity transformed Chamberlain into a figure of national significance: "Radical Joe," with his sharp, clean-cut features, his orchid and eyeglass, his impeccable attire and, apparently, his equally impeccable progressive principles. Like other radical leaders who seem as if they mean business (Lloyd George and Tony Benn, for example) he was also smeared – in his case, for his alleged republicanism and atheism. And he was denounced as a "monopoliser and dictator," a foe of Tory "freedom." Never one to turn the other cheek, Chamberlain gave his detractors as good as he got – rather like Lloyd George four decades later, during the controversy over the People's Budget of 1909.

In 1876 Chamberlain entered the House of Commons, and almost immediately set about reorganising the Liberal Party through the establishment of the National Liberal Federation in 1877 – thus provoking accusations that he was introducing American-style "caucus" politics into Britain. In 1880, after the Liberals had won a handsome victory in the general election, Chamberlain's position as a leader of the radical wing of the party was reluctantly recognised by Gladstone who offered him a seat in the cabinet as President of the Board of Trade. Despite holding a ministerial portfolio which did not in itself enable him to blaze dramatically through the political atmosphere of 1880–85, Chamberlain had managed by the summer of 1885 to promote the "Radical Programme," printed in booklet form and the first campaign handbook in British political history.

While the items of the Radical Programme had surfaced gradually over two years, a major measure of franchise reform had been forced through parliament. The Reform Act, 1884, gave the vote to hundreds of thousands of agricultural labourers, in Ireland as well as the rest of the United Kingdom. In 1885, a Redistribution Act set up mainly single-member constituencies. Franchise reform and Chamberlain's Radical Programme went together hand in glove. Enfranchised rural voters must be won over for radicalism; this in turn would strengthen Chamberlain's hand in his bid to refashion the political structure, to dispense with the Whiggish element in the Liberal alliance, and to make moderates choose between the right and the left wing of the party. In the process, Chamberlain's claims for the leadership of the purified, advanced Liberals would be rendered irresistible.

Did Chamberlain want more than this? Certainly he wanted social justice – the civic gospel recast on a national scale. Was the Radical Programme, as it was claimed, "the death knell of the laissez-faire system," an exercise in socialist confiscation and redistribution?

Despite the abuse which descended upon Chamberlain at this time, and despite the strong and provocative political language that he employed to expound his views, there is little doubt that he was trying to preserve private enterprise and private property, rather than destroy them. Disliking the strident and, as he saw it, menacing tones of marxist socialism, Chamberlain strove to make more acceptable the unacceptable face of late Victorian capitalism.

The main planks in the Radical Programme were provocative enough:

Free elementary education. Land reform, including: measures to help increase the numbers of those able to own land; the taxation of sporting, uncultivated and unoccupied land; the provision of allotments and small holdings by local authorities (who could call on compulsory powers to carry out these reforms); the enfranchisement of leaseholds; higher rates for large landed estates, and a progressive income tax on the amount of land held. Various financial reforms to aid the poor at the expense of the rich – for example, a marked increase in the proportion of direct as opposed to indirect taxation, and the encouragement of local government housing and improvement schemes (which would involve an increase in the rates). The promotion of more efficient local government through the establishment of county councils. The creation of National Councils in Dublin and Edinburgh to manage certain domestic matters. In the longer term, some items like the disestablishment of the Church of England, manhood suffrage, and the payment of MPS.

These were proposals calculated to infuriate Whig and Tory alike. Among Chamberlain's colleagues, Hartington and George Goschen were quick to criticise him, and he gave them, and others, a glorious opening when in a speech on 5 January 1885 he propounded his theory of "ransom" – asking, "What ransom will property pay for the security it enjoys?" Chamberlain provided his own answer by explaining that "Society owes a compensation to the poorer classes of this country, that it ought to recognise that claim and pay for it." In other words, welfare and reform would provide an insurance policy for privilege and property. These Fabian tactics hardly mark Chamberlain out as the Trotsky of Gladstone's second administration. Indeed, he was anxious to point out that he was "putting the rights of property on the only firm and defensible basis . . . I believe that the danger to property lies in its abuse."

During the general election campaign in the autumn of 1885, Chamberlain – to the open admiration of the young Lloyd George and Ramsay MacDonald – commended the Radical Programme to the enlarged electorate, claiming that "the great problem of our civilisation is still unsolved. We have to account for and to grapple with the mass of misery and destitution in our midst, co-existent as it is with the evidence of abundant wealth and teeming prosperity."

Chamberlain's chief bid for the agricultural workers' vote – a proposal to make allotments and smallholdings available to them through local authority funds – was encapsulated in the slogan, "Three acres and a cow." When the election results were declared, the acres and the cow had helped the Liberals to win 335 seats, thus giving them a majority of 86 over the Conservatives. The Irish Nationalists had also won 86 seats. This meant they could put the Liberals in power and keep them there. The Home Rule crisis that now ensued ended with the fall of Gladstone's government in July 1886, following the defection of Chamberlain and the Liberal Unionists over the Irish issue. Apart from the minority government of 1892–95, the Liberals were destined not to return to power until December 1905. In these circumstances, Chamberlain's plans for social reform embodied in the Radical (sometimes called "Unauthorised") Programme were doomed. The irony was that Chamberlain had been instrumental in splitting the Liberals over Irish Home Rule just as the party seemed to have become, largely through the appeal of his policies, the natural party of government.

Chamberlain spent nearly a decade in the political wilderness, returning to office only in 1895 as one of a handful of Liberal Unionist ministers in Lord Salisbury's third administration. What had happened to "Radical Joe" during this interlude? Alienated from mainstream Gladstonian Liberalism, and perturbed by the economic depression that characterised the last quarter of the 19th century, Chamberlain shifted his thinking on the means, not the desirability, of achieving social reform. Instead of redistributing wealth and taxing the prosperous middle classes, he decided to espouse the causes of economic growth and imperial consolidation.

Here was the genesis of Chamberlain's great tariff reform campaign of the early Edwardian period. Tariff reform, steering between the harsh orthodoxy of free trade and the potentially crippling effects of full-blooded economic protection, became increasingly Chamberlain's panacea for his country's ills. Selective import controls would encourage full employment at home and stimulate trade with the empire (especially with the white self-governing colonies). This would provide sufficient revenue through indirect taxation to finance a programme of social reform – in particular, old age pensions. Chamberlain's energies were directed more and more towards tariff reform in the aftermath of the Boer war (called "Chamberlain's war" by his enemies), which bled the Treasury white and gave the Unionist government a respectable reason for postponing action on old age pensions.

Tariff reform, however, with its implications of higher food prices, was rejected by the public at the 1906 general election which returned the Liberals with their last great majority. A few months after this debacle, Chamberlain suffered the stroke which left him crippled and unable to speak with any clarity. He lingered on, confined to his wheelchair, until his death a day after the news broke of the assassination of the Archduke Ferdinand at Sarajevo in 1914.

Chamberlain's ideas did not, however, die with him. The Unionist Party, within which the Liberal Unionists became increasingly indistinguishable from their Conservative allies, had clung to tariff reform as a drowning man clutches at a spar during the years of Chamberlain's infirmity. Tariff reform, after all, with its promise of extra revenue to finance necessary measures of social improvement was one of the few positive policies the party had. The Unionist commitment to tariff reform was, moreover, at least a step towards a belated Conservative recognition that a serious effort to deal with social distress was necessary.

Not that the espousal of tariff reform did them much good. When Baldwin went to the country in 1923 with this policy (though somewhat disguised as imperial preference) as the main plank in his platform, the result was the return of the first minority Labour government. It was not until 1932 that the National Government, led by Ramsay MacDonald, finally gave substance to the last of Chamberlain's great schemes to improve both the nation's trade balance and the living conditions of its people.

There was another link between the introduction of imperial preferences in 1932 and Joseph Chamberlain. The Chancellor of the Exchequer who supervised the necessary fiscal adjustments was Neville Chamberlain, Joseph's second son. Both Austen, the elder son, and Neville were devoted to the memory and to the policies of their dominating father. Austen – who in F.E. Smith's tart judgement, "always played the game and always lost it" – did his best to promote the cause of tariff reform after Chamberlain's stroke in 1906. He has been described as clearly recognising "the implication of social reform inherent in the campaign for protection, and he never looked upon a tariff as a purely financial measure."

Austen, however, spent most of his later public career involved with foreign or Indian policy making. It was Neville, who was most clearly the chief standard-bearer of the Chamberlain tradition. Leaving aside the controversy that still surrounds the Munich agreement and the appeasement of the fascist dictators, Neville Chamberlain has a remarkable record as a social reformer in the 1920s and 1930s. Like his father he was practical, and anxious to get things done. He had a healthy appetite for administrative reorganisation.

A.J.P. Taylor thinks that "nearly all the achievements of Conservative government between the wars stand to his credit," and certainly the list of his administrative reforms are impressive. His Housing Act, 1923, was meant to stimulate both public and private house-building. He was a creative and compassionate Minister of Health under Bonar Law and Baldwin. He reformed local government, doing "more to improve it than any man in the 20th century." His Unemployment Act, 1934, rationalised the chaos of unemployment relief.

Neville Chamberlain believed that poverty should be remedied by government action. This had not hitherto been a belief characteristic of Conservative ministers, but at least it produced a belated fulfilment, and on a national scale, of some of Joseph Chamberlain's progressive but non-socialist remedies for alleviating poverty and distress. In this sense, Joseph Chamberlain, through Neville's achievements, can be seen as one of the architects of the Conservative Party's grudging acceptance of the modern welfare state.

It is an intriguing footnote to this story that it could well have been the Labour Party that Joseph Chamberlain influenced instead. In 1884, when he was at the height of his influence in the Liberal Party, Chamberlain, once more a widower, paid heavy-handed court to Beatrice Potter, the future Mrs Sidney Webb of early Fabianism. But Chamberlain made hardly any allowances for Beatrice Potter's blue-stockinged independence of mind, and she discovered him to be an "enthusiast and a despot."

Yet, despite her disinclination to be dominated intellectually by Chamberlain, Beatrice fell passionately, if fitfully, in love with him, responding to his "energy and personal magnetism, in a word masculine force to an almost superlative degree." Of a masterful temperament herself Beatrice was not, however, prepared to become Chamberlain's dutiful platform wife. In 1891, she became engaged to Sidney Webb, remarking resignedly that it seemed "an extraordinary end for the once brilliant Beatrice Potter . . . to marry an ugly little man with no social position and less means . . . And I am not 'in love,' not as I was."

There was to be no enduring link between the great leader of the radical Liberals and one of the inspirers of the British labour movement.

OCTAVIA HILL
1838–1912

Peter Malpass

Paradise Place, Marylebone, was a wholly unremarkable London slum, dilapidated, insanitary and seriously overcrowded. But in 1865 it became the starting point for a novel experiment in housing management which soon established Octavia Hill as a leading authority on housing for the poor.

Contemporary admirers liked to rank her alongside figures such as Florence Nightingale, as one of the greatest women of the 19th century. Besides her distinctive approach to housing management, Octavia Hill was influential in other ways. She was, for instance, a leading lobbyist behind the Artisans' and Labourers' Dwellings Improvement Act, 1875 (the Cross Act), and she gave evidence before the Royal Commission on the Housing of the Working Classes in 1884. But her interests went far beyond housing. In 1868 she was involved at the start of a body called the London Association for the Prevention of Pauperisation and Crime, which was the forerunner of the Charity Organisation Society. She remained very closely identified with the society for many years, and therefore has a claim to be one of the founders of modern social work. She was also one of the leaders of the campaign to etablish the National Trust. And in her later years she was, with Beatrice Webb, a member of the Royal Commission on the Poor Laws, 1905–09.

In the years since her death in 1912, the continuing relevance of her ideas and methods has been seriously questioned. But there is no doubt that she did play an important role in helping to establish and systematise the practice of social work and housing management. It was in housing, in fact, that she made her most original contribution, and it is here that she retains her status. Most writers on housing management still refer to her pioneering work, often implying that she established modern housing management principles almost single-handed.

When she began her housing work in 1865, Octavia Hill was 27 years old, a young woman of middle class upbringing, but by no means wealthy. Her grandfather was Dr Thomas Southwood Smith, a public health reformer. Her father had been a corn and wool merchant until a complete collapse in his health ended his business career when he still had a large family of children. So, from an early age, she had to earn her own living, and she did not approach charitable work from a position of personal financial security. Indeed, she was led into it by the discoveries she made about the lives of the poor while she was employed as the supervisor of a toy-making workroom for Ragged School children. Nonetheless, it was her unshakeable belief in the moral superiority of the middle and upper classes which gave her the confidence for her housing management project.

What aroused her passion and interest were the difficulties poor families with children had in getting decent accommodation. Landlords of decent property were reluctant to take tenants with children, especially if they came from poorer areas. Yet in the slums themselves, the behaviour of the landlords was, she felt, a major factor in creating the squalor and uhealthy conditions in which children had to grow up. In the slums, absentee landlords would farm out the tasks of letting and rent collection to middle men or women, who were often impoverished slum dwellers themselves. There was a rapid turnover of tenants, and the moonlight flit was a common way of avoiding the rent. Bad debts were an accepted hazard. This tempted landlords to compensate by setting rents at a high level, and by neglecting to carry out even essential repairs. To the problems of overcrowding caused by poverty and high rents were added the problems of broken windows, leaking roofs and blocked drains.

However, Octavia Hill believed that the tenants were *equally* to blame for the existence of slums. She saw slum tenants as irresponsible, drunken, feckless, and content to live in squalor. In her evidence to the Royal Commission on the Housing of the Working Classes she repeatedly referred to the "destructive and criminal classes," and she said that she believed the destructive class to be very numerous in London. Elsewhere she wrote: "The people's homes are bad, partly because they are badly built and arranged; they are tenfold worse because the tenants' habits and lives are what they are. Transplant them tomorrow to healthy and commodious homes and they would pollute and destroy them" (*Homes of the London Poor*, 1875).

It was at this chaotic end of the housing market that she deliberately chose to operate. Other attempts were made to provide decent housing for the working class. But the charitable foundations and model-dwellings companies failed to break the seemingly inevitable link between poverty and bad housing. By building *new* housing, these enterprises incurred costs which, despite the low rate of interest they charged, resulted in rents that only the better-paid skilled artisans could afford. Only Octavia Hill aimed to reach the truly poor – that section of the population whom she described as being "as low a class as have a settled abode." (Even she did not help those who lived on the streets or in common lodging houses.)

She tried to induce order out of the confusion by enlightened management, of both the property and the tenants. She restructured and redefined the landlord-tenant relationship, seeking to achieve improved living conditions without excessive rents. Instead of new buildings, she believed that better management of *existing* accommodation was the way to help the poor. She wanted to redeem the people of the slums from what she saw as their destructive ways. The starting point on the route to thrift, sobriety and responsibility was a strict insistence on prompt payment of rent.

Octavia Hill claimed that she *never* allowed arrears of rent. But in return for regular payments by the tenants, she gave a guarantee that she would fulfil her obligations as landlord. The landlord-tenant relationship should be based on reciprocal obligations. The tenant could see that regular payment of rent resulted in repair and improvement to the house, thereby raising his standard of living. As the tenant acquired the habit of paying his rent regularly, and as he grew accustomed to better living conditions, Octavia Hill believed he would develop a generally more responsive attitude. If he did not show signs of responding, she was quite prepared to evict.

Lacking capital of her own, she was from the outset the manager of other people's property. So profitability was important. Her early patron was John Ruskin, who urged her to pay 5 per cent per annum on capital invested in her scheme. He predicted that, if she could achieve this rate of return, and show that it was a paying proposition, then the work would expand. She later claimed that she was never short of people willing to buy houses for her to manage.

Her attempts to improve her tenants went far beyond regular rent collection and fixing of repairs. She became involved in all aspects of their lives. She used her powerful position as landlord to engage their enthusiasm or secure their cooperation. Her initiatives took various forms. She provided a kind of community room for her first tenants in a cleaned-out stable behind her own house, and she secured a patch of open ground as a play area for the children. On the other hand, she could be coercive. She threatened to evict a man who would not send his children to school.

To Hill, housing management meant patient and firm education of the poor in how to lead better lives, as defined by the values of the middle and upper classes. This distinguished her approach from both the commercial management style of the up-market capitalist landlords, and the chaotic non-management style of the down-market slum-owners. Her status as a pioneer rests on her attempt to create order in the administration of dwellings occupied by people who were widely regarded as irretrievably feckless, and still show a return on investment. Her originality lay in the way she combined the role of landlord with middle class outreach to the poor. The key to understanding her approach is that she made housing management into a form of social work.

The idea that the poor could be rescued from moral turpitude by the personal commitment of their social superiors had been around for some years before she made the imaginative leap which combined this commitment with the role of landlord. She and her colleagues in the Charity Organisation Society were much influenced by the writings of Thomas Chalmers (1780–1847), who had urged that individual character was the main cause of social distress, and that the indiscriminate distribution of charity harmed the recipient by breeding despondency. The COS grew out of a concern with the unsystematic expansion of charitable donations to the poor during the 1860s. It was a response to Chalmers's teaching that true charity was that which helped to make the recipient independent of the giver. Her idea that the rich had a duty to assist the poor through personal contact and example had earlier led to the creation of "visiting societies." Both the COS and Octavia Hill's housing management were within this tradition. The system of regular rent collection by middle class ladies was a form of social work designed primarily to create that personal relationship which was judged to be the basis of moral redemption. Within the COS, emphasis was placed on the importance of careful investigation of each case, so that help could be given in an appropriate form – ie, in a form which cultivated independence. For Hill and the COS, charity was properly concerned with more than the relief of poverty. It was about personal improvement and the prevention of pauperisation. Fear of pauperisation seems to have blinded them to the problem of poverty itself.

The Octavia Hill system of housing management was a highly labour-intensive and time-consuming activity. She began to recruit and train a growing number of middle class ladies as volunteer rent collectors and property managers. The young Beatrice Potter, before her marriage to Sidney Webb, worked for a time in the mid-1880s as one of these housing managers in the East End of London. She found it not only very hard work but also, for her, a radicalising experience.

The block of dwellings where she worked had been built by the East End Dwellings Company, a reminder that it was not just individual investors who entrusted their property to Miss Hill's care but also corporate bodies. Most notable among these were the Ecclesiastical Commissioners who handed over the management of a considerable number of dwellings in Southwark and Deptford. As the number of dwellings offered to Octavia Hill increased, she adopted a decentralised system with very little direct control over the volunteer helpers. (Beatrice Webb later wrote that she had only met Octavia Hill once whilst working as a housing manager, and that was over dinner.) She told the Royal Commission in 1884 that she did not know how many trained workers she had, nor how many dwellings were managed according to her principles.

She was so opposed to any state interference with the market mechanism (she believed that any subsidy would simply lower wages) that she was forced to defend minimal standards of provision for the poor. She thought that a family with two tiny children needed only one room. It was her normal practice to encourage families to occupy only the space that they could afford to pay for on a regular basis, regardless of their needs. In relation to new building she pleaded for simplicity: "Primarily, I should not carry the water and the drains all over the place; I think that is ridiculous. If you have water on every floor that is quite sufficient for working people . . . Of course the same thing applies to the drains, and it is not the least necessary that they should be laid everywhere."

A further quotation reveals her attitude to her tenants: "I do not say that I will not have drunkards, I have quantities of drunkards; but everything depends upon whether I think the drunkard will be better for being sent away or not. *It is a tremendous despotism* [my italics], but it is exercised with a view of bringing out the powers of the people, and treating them as responsible for themselves within certain limits." Her approach was blatantly authoritarian. But it was an authoritarianism based on faith in the superiority of her class and the belief that the poor must be trained to lead better lives. As in her work with the COS the targets for her despotism were the *deserving poor*.

As a strong believer in the individualist philosophy Octavia Hill not only placed great reliance on the ability of private charity and the personal commitment of wealthy people to bring about social change, but she also fiercely opposed further state intervention. In particular, she was firmly against any kind of state subsidy or state provision of housing. Public housing, which was being pioneered by the London County Council from the 1890s, was anathema.

Octavia Hill was undeniably one of the leading figures in the production of a particular kind of alternative to the Poor Law. She has a genuine claim to be one of the pioneers of both housing management and social work. In particular, her emphasis on establishing close relationships with individuals and families in need has formed the basis of a continuing tradition in social work and retains its relevance in housing.

However, the form of housing management which she devised has played only a minor part in the development of modern practice. Whereas she opposed state intervention and relied on women volunteers to work closely with tenants, it is council housing, run in a bureaucratic fashion by a salaried professional group dominated by men, which has become the main setting for the management of rented housing. Despite Octavia Hill's valuable pioneering work in this field, housing management was, in effect, reinvented in the 1920s as a wholly administrative activity centred on local government and lacking the moralistic overtones of her method.

She was essentially a moral crusader and an innovator whose views attracted considerable support at the time. In her own lifetime, however, her relentless adherence to the individualist faith was being overtaken by the rising tide of collectivism which reached its height in the late 1940s. It is only now that the tide is beginning to run her way as basic assumptions about welfare services in modern Britain are challenged by the economic crisis and a government pledged to roll back the state. The political and intellectual climate is today more sympathetic to the kinds of ideas promoted by Octavia Hill than at any time for at least a generation.

CHARLES BOOTH
1840–1916

Philip Waller

Charles Booth ensured a lasting reputation with the publication of the social survey, the *Life and Labour of the People in London*, a monumental work in 17 volumes which appeared between 1889 and 1903. The exact origin of Booth's inquiry, however, is not easy to determine. As with many famous expeditions, romance has gathered about it. The estimate of the marxist Social Democratic Federation, in 1885, that some 25 per cent of the London working class suffered extreme poverty, allegedly provoked Booth to inaugurate his own survey, with a view to confounding the claim as gross exaggeration. But a case can be made for lighting upon 1883 as the critical year for Booth, owing to the coincidental issue of three publications, Robert Giffen's essay, "The Progress of the Working Classes in the last Half-Century," the Rev. Andrew Mearns's pamphlet, *The Bitter Cry of Outcast London*, and the reports of the 1881 census. Each had an important bearing on that subject, the social condition of the people, whose investigation was to occupy Booth for over two decades.

Some preliminary comment is advisable, however, about Booth's reputation, the character of the man and his work, before undertaking a review of his achievement. Pioneer of the empirical school of English sociology and progenitor of state-bequeathed old age pensions, Charles Booth nonetheless is probably better perceived as eminent Victorian than founder of the welfare state. It is sobering, when contemplating intellectual enterprise and courage on this scale, to reflect on the degree to which Booth remained prisoner of contemporary conventions. Not that Booth ever felt the need to apologise for this: he was convinced that certain values were absolute, that certain standards of personal conduct were correct, and that certain systems of economic organisation were superior.

Booth's writing is conspicuous for two features, apparently contradictory – detachment and moralising. Conscious of variable levels of reality and experience, he coolly measured social circumstances while all the time puzzling about the nature of a disposing providence. It is well to establish at the outset this moral emphasis in Booth. It was never subordinated to mere measurement as he laboured to define the condition of his day. Moreover, in party-political preference, Booth was a Unionist at the time he undertook his inquiry into the life and labour of the people.

Here, it seems, are paradoxes. They invite the question: How did this ship-owner and merchant turn himself into the author of a mammoth social survey? But the question is unreal. No conversion took place. Booth added one career to another. He never ceased to think and perform as a captain of industry.

Note, for instance, his considered view of cyclical unemployment, expressed in 1903 upon completion of his poverty study. Aware, more than most, of the social hardships which unemployment brought, he remained alert to business needs. His final judgment was not dissimilar to the orthodox character-building school, confident in capitalism's self-adjusting capacity. From some points of view, he wrote, "these cycles of depression have a distinctly harmful and even a cruel aspect; but from a more distant point of view, 'afar from the sphere of our sorrow,' they seem less malignant . . . There are some victims, but those who are able and willing to provide in times of prosperity for the lean years which seem inevitably to follow, do not suffer at all; and, if the alternation of good and bad times be not too sudden or too great, the community gains not only be the strengthening of character under stress, but also by a direct effect on enterprise."

Born in Liverpool in 1840, Charles Booth was the third son of a corn merchant. With his eldest brother, Alfred, he built up a successful steamship company. He remained an active chairman of the company until 1912, four years before his death. The commercial community in which he worked deeply influenced his social attitudes, because it was a community joined not just in business but in marriage and in religious and charitable endeavours.

Booth's family connections were extensive, within and without Liverpool. When he married Mary Macaulay, niece of the historian, in 1871, he was attached to a signal intellectual aristocracy. Not least among his acquired relations was Beatrice Potter, better known as Beatrice Webb. She assisted Booth in his first survey of London poverty and industry; but a distance grew between them when her incipient socialism became pronounced upon her marriage to Sidney Webb in 1892. Booth's and Beatrice Webb's subsequent difficult association, as colleagues on the Royal Commission on the Poor Laws (1905–9), only served to underline how divergent their views on social organisation had become.

The religious circle into which Booth was born was Unitarian – a self-consciously tolerant, philanthropic sect, whose stress on social service sustained them in the absence of spiritual certainty. Booth also toiled with positivism, meeting it through the advocacy of his cousins, Albert and Henry Crompton. But their confidence never elicited more than passing subscription from Booth himself. Without settled belief, Booth nonetheless remained sure of the importance of the spiritual side of man.

The quest to comprehend it occupied a significant portion of the *Life and Labour* – seven out of the 17 volumes, in all. By general consent, this "Religious Influences" section is the least satisfactory. It was an unbalanced and incomplete account of the "moral question," because most people were untouched by the religious agencies whose activities he sought to appraise. For Booth himself, this undertaking was a spiritual voyage. It ended almost an obsession. Most of the reports were personal distillations, the record of his own attendances at umpteen religious services. They contain an amount of fascinating evidence and supposition – about the social class nature of formal worship, for instance. "It is respectability that causes people to go to church," Booth drily observed, "far more than it is church-going that makes them respectable." The impressionistic nature of this survey, however, meant that a good deal of its comment throws more light on the personality of Booth than on the social environment which was ostensibly the object of his study. The "Religious Influences" series did not, then, establish a secure method for the sociology of religion. Description and evaluation were uneasily combined, and the concentration on organised religion left out of account the wider ambit of spiritual expression and satisfaction.

Life, not surprisingly, proved less decipherable to Booth than labour. Here the twin impulses which made up his motivation – search for a personal meaning to existence, and for satisfaction from business enterprise – coalesced to furnish inspiration for study. Poverty, material and moral, was shockingly exhibited in Liverpool, where Booth lived for the first 33 years of his life. Initially, his views on politics and public policy were conventionally Liberal. Booth welcomed the extension of the franchise as a step towards self-government, although involvement in Liberal ward politics brought disenchantment. Public education seemed another means to this end, and he supported the Education League's programme. Disappointment followed with the Education Act, 1870, and the demonstration of sectarian jealousies. But Booth never lost his faith in education as a vehicle of progress.

Booth was not unsympathetic to tax-payers' yearning for economy, but he refused to convict school boards of "extravagance." On the contrary, "it was worth much to carry high the flag of education." Mixing his metaphors, he affirmed that every "school stands up from its playground like a church in God's acre ringing its bell."

Booth never lost faith in the capitalist system. Free enterprise, on the whole, tended towards personal fulfilment and national progress. Socialism was an artificial, injurious scheme which struck at those qualities which Booth prized most highly, independence and mutuality – or what he termed "the exercise of faculty" and "the interchange of service." Awareness of poverty amid plenty never led him to conclude that the resourcefulness of capitalism was exhausted, or that its basic premises were fallacious – though he was apprehensive that capitalism was now on trial. "From helpless feelings," he wrote in 1886, "spring socialistic theories, passionate suggestions of ignorance, setting at naught the nature of man and neglecting all the fundamental facts of human existence."

What were intelligent and responsible businessmen to do in these circumstances? It was useless, also immoral, to contemplate surrendering wealth. Wealth entailed obligations as well as providing privileges: "It would be a breach of the very trust on which we hold it, and as cowardly as the flight of old from the world into a monastery." The thing was to gain clear-sightedness about what exactly were the shortcomings in current industrial organisation, in social arrangements and in personal behaviour, and to remain steadfast to certain goals, the chief of which was the enlargement of personal independence.

Booth's advocacy of old age pensions in the 1890s was cast in these terms: they would guarantee a "security of position which will stimulate, rather than weaken, the play of individuality on which progress and prosperity depend." The precondition, however, was knowledge about what it was which reduced so many people to the sorry plight which required remedial action.

Booth was not without Victorian optimism in the beneficent power of information, but his appetite for facts was never just accumulative or aimless. On the contrary, his thoughts were directed towards particular problems: Who were the poor? Why were they poor? How did the anomaly arise of industry's coexistence with poverty, when Booth took it as axiomatic that "where there is industry there ought to be no poverty"? Then, when the facts were established, what interpretation should be placed on them, and what course of public policy should be pursued? Especially, "can the central action of the state, or the interference of local government, either increase the total volume of enterprise or beneficially regulate its flow?"

The formulation of Booth's inquiry was a natural progression from the debates of the 1880s. Booth was not alone in being alarmed by the emergence of socialist propaganda. A counter existed already. Robert Giffen's presidential address to the Statistical Society in 1883, "The Progress of the Working Classes in the last Half-Century," generated widespread interest. Its morals were those to which Booth could hardly fail to respond. "Vast improvement" had derived from the capitalist economic regime – "the 'poor' have had almost all the benefit of the great material advance of the last 50 years." The nation ought to proceed further along the same lines, conceding nothing in the war with the "land nationaliser and socialist."

"Take away the rewards," Giffen warned, "and even the best would probably not give themselves up to doing what the community wants and now pays them for doing, but they would give themselves up either to idleness or to doing something else."

A senior official at the Board of Trade, Giffen was no Pangloss. "No one can can contemplate the present condition of the masses," he wrote, "without desiring something like a revolution for the better." The trouble was that no one could contemplate Giffen's statistical work without also desiring something better. The admission that his working class "included every man who works" was damaging and liable to discredit an otherwise cogent thesis. This admission emerged during discussion of Giffen's follow-up paper, delivered to the Statistical Society in March 1886.

Students of the Booth inquiry have insufficiently stressed the significance of the Giffen controversy. They are on firmer ground when they note the reception which the Statistical Society in 1887 accorded Booth's paper, "The Inhabitants of Tower Hamlets (School Board Division), their Condition and Occupations," in particular a series of testing questions put to Booth by Professor Leone Levi. This inter-rogation stimulated Booth to crystallise his objectives.

Sensational literature about the condition of the masses – *The Bitter Cry of Outcast London* and its imitators – dissatisfied Booth by its gaudy, unscientific projection of "terrible pictures: starving children, suffering women, overworked men; horrors of drunkenness and vice, monsters and demons of inhumanity; giants of disease and despair. Did these pictures truly represent what lay behind, or did they bear to the facts a relation similar to that which the pictures outside a booth at some country fair bear to the performance or show within?" Scepticism about philanthropic endeavours and suspicion of socialist nostrums alike offended that disciplined cast of mind in which business practice had schooled him. Herein lay the circumstantial causes of Booth's great inquiry, though we should not ignore the element of personal therapy which permeates the entire undertaking. Booth was not rudderless, but his life took on fresh meaning when he embarked on his odyssey.

Preparatory work had been done already by Booth in examination of the censuses. The 1881 census reports were published in 1883. The first paper which Booth read to the Statistical Society, "Occupations of the People of the United Kingdom, 1841–81," aimed to rearrange the data in order to facilitate comparisons and to document social and economic change. The task was plagued by the "want of fixity of principle or method as between succeeding censuses." Subsequently he served on an advisory committee which pressed on the Registrar-General for the 1891 census new terms of reference "by which the position and manner of life of each family could be measured." The most important was the index of overcrowding.

Not content to wait on official agencies, Booth determined to cut his own path through the wilderness, to indicate "the numerical relation which poverty, misery, and depravity bear to regular earnings and comparative comfort, and to describe the general conditions under which each class lives." He supposed that, though dispersed, the information was not altogether elusive. Organisation could supply the coherence needed, and organisation was the forte of the successful businessman like Booth.

Census data were supplemented by umpteen other sources of information over the 16 years of Booth's inquiry. It was Joseph Chamberlain who, through Beatrice Webb, gave Booth the idea of using the notebooks of London School Board attendance officers, some 400 persons with intimate knowledge of each district and its working class families. Booth added to this account by wholesale interviewing of the school board visitors themselves, Boards of Guardians and relieving officers, teachers, police, sanitary and factory inspectors, rate collectors, trade union and friendly society officials, charity workers, hospital almoners, clergy, some employers, and miscellaneous individuals, some of whom Booth lodged with periodically.

Booth's investment of time and energy was prodigious. He was also the impresario of a talented team whose members undertook special assignments. In addition to Beatrice Webb, several were outstanding. Ernest Aves (1857–1917), a graduate of Cambridge, and Hubert Llewellyn Smith (1864–1945), of Oxford, were both drawn from Toynbee Hall. Aves was afterwards chairman of Trade Boards, Llewellyn Smith permanent under-secretary at the Board of Trade, and director of the sequel to Booth, the *New Survey of London Life and Labour*, 1928–35.

The result of their joint endeavours was, as *The Times* declared of the 1891 publication, "the grimmest book of our generation." The marxist estimate of London poverty was not overturned, but confirmed. But what – seen with hindsight – were the shortcomings of

Booth's inquiry and what should be considered its achievements?

Some of the shortcomings were explicit. The work was confined, Booth acknowledged, "to the description of things as they are. I have not undertaken to investigate how they came to be so, nor, except incidentally, to indicate whither they are tending . . ."

The comprehensive coverage which was Booth's aim was probably misplaced. The statistical technique of sampling, later applied by A.L. Bowley, would have spared Booth much strenuous effort. Furthermore, it was a naive presumption to think that the facts, upon discovery, could speak for themselves. Booth's eventual organisation of the facts, with a view to prescribing public action on social policy, was influenced in part by an *a priori* moral position which bore no obvious relation to his research discoveries. He was especially concerned to underline qualitative distinctions between the very poor and the working class.

His system of classification was designed to isolate this problem. In class A were grouped the loafers and the criminals, and in class B the most degraded casual workers. These were the "very poor" (8.4 per cent of the population). Those with intermittent and small regular earnings, his classes C and D (22.3 per cent), constituted "the poor." Those with regular standard earnings and the higher class of labour, classes E and F (51.5 per cent), were placed above the poverty line.

Alarmed by the manner in which character deteriorated under casual labour, Booth early reached this conclusion: "The entire removal of this class (A and B) out of the daily struggle for existence I believe to be the only solution of the problem of poverty." They should be sent off to labour colonies. The severity of this remedy was not peculiar to Booth. It appealed broadly as a means of relieving and spurring to self-improvement the classes above: "To the rich the very poor are a sentimental interest: to the poor they are a crushing load. The poverty of the poor is mainly the result of the competition of the very poor."

If this draconian aspect was all there was to Booth he might be passed over as simply the ablest of the unimaginative school who equated cruelty with kindness. The constructive side of Booth, though constrained by convention, was real enough. "Limited socialism" was his famous recipe, designed to assist "those who cannot stand alone." This was "a socialism which shall leave untouched the forces of individualism and the sources of wealth." In practice, it fell not far short of the "minimum standards" philosophy of the welfare state.

Booth's advocacy of old age pensions was as a right of citizenship by public endowment, rather than as a contributory insurance scheme available only to select groups. His study of Stepney had inclined him to the view that old age was responsible for perhaps a third of the cases of pauperism. Hence his championship of a pension to enhance the old person's dignity and independence. Five shillings a week at the age of 65, as Booth proposed, was not a living pension, rather a supplement to personal savings or family aid. But the universality of the endowment incorporated a novel political concept, and the cost was bound to create new adventures in budgetary provision. Booth's service as a member of the Royal Commission on the Aged Poor (1892–95) gave him the chance to promote this cause. Though the politics of the question were beyond his bidding, the scheme which was eventually introduced by Lloyd George in 1908–9 owed something to his work.

In respect of organisation of the labour market, too, Booth's findings and advocacy exercised an influence, in the direction of de-casualisation and on William Beveridge's implementation of labour exchanges. Most of all, Booth's achievement was felt in the stimulus he gave to others to explore, document, and analyse the condition of the people. Two classics of the late Victorian and Edwardian period, Seebohm Rowntree's *Poverty: a study of town life* (1901) and Lady Bell's *At the Works* (1907), were obvious outgrowths from Booth's work. Lady Bell, indeed, dedicated her book "to Charles Booth, of wise and sympathetic counsel."

This identifies his most impressive attribute, his equability. He disturbed complacency in the most agreeable fashion. His work could not be dismissed. The research was impregnable. He described and invited others to face a problem which was immense, but Booth's unflappable temperament made it – indeed his commitment to capitalism obliged him to make it – seem a manageable problem. He could not be passed over as a hysterical revolutionary.

His impact was all the greater *because* he belonged to the governing classes and aimed to preserve the existing system. The regime vindicated itself in Booth's humanity.

EBENEZER HOWARD
1850–1928

Peter Hall

If it is the fate of great original thinkers to be misunderstood, then evidently Ebenezer Howard was one. Almost everyone seems to have got him wrong. People think that he advocated low-density housing; in fact, his garden city would have had densities more like inner London's. They mix up his garden city with the garden suburb found first in Hampstead and then in countless Metroland imitations, which was its opposite. If they understand, they visualise a small isolated town deep in the countryside, whereas Howard foresaw planned agglomerations with perhaps millions of people. Most fundamentally, they think of Howard as a physical planner, ignoring that his plan was in fact an astonishing blueprint for the total reconstruction of society.

They cannot claim that Howard made it difficult. In his 78-year life he wrote but one book, and that a very slim one. First published in 1898 as *To-morrow: A Peaceful Path to Real Reform*, it was reissued in 1902 with the title that made it famous, *Garden Cities of To-morrow*. This second edition did have two unfortunate features, which have dogged the book in all subsequent appearances.

First, it truncated one of the most important diagrams, that showed Howard's total vision of the planned agglomeration or Social City – a defect remedied only 70 years later, when the Open University put the original full-colour version on one of its covers. Second, and more seriously, its new title succeeded in diverting attention away from the truly radical nature of Howard's ideas, demoting him from social visionary into physical planner.

To understand these ideas, some biography is needed. Contrary to popular belief, Howard was not a "planner." He spent almost his whole career as a shorthand reporter in the Law Courts: a job that paid him little but presumably allowed his thoughts to roam. The exception came early. Born in 1850, the son of a shopkeeper in the City of London – a fact commemorated in a plaque, ironically at the very edge of the Barbican scheme of which he would probably have disapproved – he spent much of his childhood in country towns: Sudbury, Ipswich, Cheshunt. Then at 21, he emigrated to America and became a pioneer in Nebraska. He proved no farmer, and from 1872 to 1876 earned his living as a shorthand reporter in Chicago.

Little is known about Howard's American years. But they were undoubtedly formative. He had participated for a few months in one of the greatest social experiments the world has seen: the Homestead Act of 1862, which opened up the interior of the United States to pioneer farmers free of charge. Arguably, apart from independence itself, this was the most important event in American history: it established its economic base in prosperous, middle-sized, efficient farms and small towns and its educational and cultural foundation in land grant colleges devoted to scientific agriculture and mechanical arts. Whether Howard consciously realised it or not, this experience later proved decisive – because, in fact, his book is a tract in favour of urban homesteading.

America was important in another way. Chicago, in the years Howard spent there, was rebuilding after the Great Fire of 1871. Before that, in its pre-skyscraper days, it had been known as the Garden City – almost certainly the source of Howard's name. Now, the great landscape architect Frederic Law Olmsted – designer of New York's Central Park – was building Riverside, a garden suburb outside the city. His plan derived from another – completed just before Riverside – for the new campus town of Berkeley in California. Almost certainly, Berkeley-Riverside was one of the physical design ideas that eventually blended into Howard's Garden City.

Back in London, Howard plunged into the intellectual ferment of the London of the 1880s. Britain was experiencing a major economic depression. Its farm workers, stricken by a flood of cheap meat and grain imported from America and Australia, poured off the land and into the overcrowded cities – to be joined by the first of a wave of immigrants from eastern Europe.

Charles Booth, who was beginning his great social survey in the East End of London, found that a quarter of the population lived below the subsistence level. The plight of the London poor exploded into strikes: the match girls in 1888, the dockers in 1889. On Bloody Sunday – 13 November 1887 – socialists and Irish home-rulers fought huge battles with the police in the centre of London, raising the spectre of civil disorder.

Against this background, Howard began to read and to write. He was quite specific, in *Garden Cities*, that he developed his central ideas for himself but that he then found other writers who supplied the bricks for his structure. From Edward Gibbon Wakefield he developed the idea of promoting colonisation for the poor. From one by-product of that idea,

Colonel Light's plan for the city of Adelaide in South Australia, he obtained the germ of the Social City: a city that reproduced itself, once it had reached a set limit, by starting a copy nearby.

From the economist, Alfred Marshall, he got the specific idea of relocating workers from London, with their industry, in towns built in the countryside. From James Silk Buckingham's plan for a model town he obtained most of the essential features of his diagrammatic plan of Garden City, including the central place, the radial avenues, the peripheral industry.

From Herbert Spencer he first borrowed the idea of land nationalisation, and then from Spencer's forgotten predecessor, Thomas Spence, he borrowed a superior variant: the notion of purchase of agricultural land by a local community, at agricultural land values – so that the increased value, arising from the construction of the town, passed not to a landlord but to the community itself.

There was a final ingredient – though in strict chronology, it seems to have provided the intellectual starting point. Edward Bellamy's *Looking Backward*, a prophetic picture of life in late 20th century Boston, was published in 1888 and immediately excited enormous attention on both sides of the Atlantic. Howard was seized by its central notion: that new technology could provide the means to liberate the worker from needless toil, creating the basis for a new cooperative order. Thus American ideas allied with American experience to provide the basis for the garden city idea.

These were the very diverse ingredients. But, as Howard rightly claimed in a chapter heading, his was a unique combination of proposals that in total proved much greater than the sum of the parts. He started with the famous diagram of the Three Magnets: archaically charming, particularly in its original coloured version, it in fact puts on one page what it would take much longer to say in modern planners' jargon. The overcrowded city and the depopulating countryside both had advantages and disadvantages: economic and social opportunity, slums and smoke on the one side; a collapsing economy coupled with cheap land and good environment on the other. The key was to combine the best of both in a new form, Town-Country or Garden City.

To this end, a group of people should borrow money to build a new town far out in the countryside, where land values were rock bottom. Industrialists should move their factories there; workers would come and build houses. The town would be kept to a fixed limit of about 32,000 people, on 1,000 acres of land – about one and a half times the City of London. It would be surrounded by a permanent green belt, also owned by the town, with farms and institutions needing a rural location. As more people and firms moved out, further new towns would be built close by, all interconnected by a rapid transit system (or, as Howard called it, an Inter-Municipal Railway). The result would be Social City; a vast planned agglomeration, almost without limit.

So it is right to say that Howard provides a physical blueprint. What is important, and what is missed, is that this is merely a key to a much more radical plan for the reconstruction of society. The key is the collective ownership by the citizens, in perpetuity, of the land. In one of the coloured diagrams of the first edition, omitted later, Howard illustrated "The Vanishing Point of Landlord's Rent": if only the community could borrow the initial capital to buy land at a sufficient distance from the great city, then it would itself create the value of land and would benefit from it. Its citizens would pay a modest rate-rent for their houses or factories or farms, which would be sufficient to repay the interest on the borrowed money, provide a sinking fund that would permit repayment of capital, and provide for all municipal needs without any need for rates or for central government help.

From this, Howard could argue that he had found a third socio-economic system, superior both to pure capitalism and to socialism. Local communal ownership of land would supply abundant resources for generous public services, creating a local welfare state, directly responsible to the citizenry. Services would be provided by the municipality, or by private contractors, as the citizens found more efficient. Yet other public services would come from voluntary action of the people, in a series of what Howard called pro-municipal experiments. In particular, the people would build their own homes in this way, through building societies, friendly societies, cooperative societies or trade unions.

Howard's vast cooperative housing programme was, however, intended to be more than just a great social experiment; it was deliberately conceived as a plan to overcome mass unemployment by providing work for all. The construction of Garden Cities was to drive the economy, as the construction of railways had done 50 or 60 years earlier. Students of Kondratieff long waves will find this advice, coming at the trough of a depression, particularly percipient. It seems clear that by the 1880s Howard had arrived at the same solution as Keynes, in the next Kondratieff trough 50 years later: society must invest its way out of the depression.

Even this was not all. The social organisation he proposed was to provide a solid basis of welfare, which would guarantee support and dignity to senior citizens and female-headed households.

But at the same time, it was systematically designed to encourage new small enterprise. It would call, he wrote, "for all kinds, of architects, artists, medical men, experts in sanitation, landscape gardeners, agricultural experts, surveyors, builders, manufacturers, merchants and financiers, organisers of trade unions, friendly and cooperative societies, as well as the very simplest forms of unskilled labour, together with all those forms of lesser skill and talent which lie between.''

There are two features that distinguish this version. The first, derived doubtless from Bellamy and from Howard's experience, is its American quality. Howard, interestingly, is free from the vice that afflicted almost all his Victorian intellectual contemporaries, as described in the penetrating recent analysis by the American historian, Martin Wiener (who unaccountably fails to consider him). Unlike them, he never rejects industry or technology or urbanism in themselves, seeing them rather as the essential means toward his alternative society. But at the same time, by freeing men and women of the burden of inherited landed wealth, Howard is able to produce a vision of free, independent and creative spirits. It is the homesteading spirit brought home to industrial England.

But it goes one step beyond that: to a vision, derived from Bellamy, of new technology bringing a new cooperative spirit based on free association. (It sounds like a Social Democratic Party document.) The most startling feature about Howard's ideas, re-read today, is their modernity. Almost all the features of latter-day British political philosophy of the left-centre brand are here: the rejection of monolithic state socialism and the stress on local collective action, the emphasis on accountability.

This, not the details of the streets and parks, is what constitutes the uniqueness of Howard's proposals – and the justification for his original title. As Lewis Mumford says in his 1946 introduction to the book, Howard is less interested in physical forms than in social processes. Garden Cities were the instruments of a new socio-economic order.

It follows that the building of the new order must come through an actual programme of construction. One brilliant feature of Howard's plan is that it could be created incrementally, by scores of local initiatives. Howard accordingly started an association – the Garden Cities Association – in 1899. Three years later, he took the lead in forming a Garden City Pioneer Company; a year after that, the First Garden City Company. Letchworth, started in that year with privately subscribed capital on a 3,800-acre site 35 miles north of London, already had 5,000 people by 1907 and 9,000 by 1914.

But, by then, his movement had already begun to show a fundamental rift – as indicated by its change of name, to the Garden Cities and Town Planning Association, in 1907. Raymond Unwin and Barry Parker, the brilliant architect-planners who had been hired to design

Letchworth, took on another commission, for Hampstead Garden Suburb, in 1907. Superficially resembling Letchworth – Unwin gave it a romantic city wall and gateways in the medieval German style, Parker and Unwin together its feel of domestic English cosiness – Hampstead was basically its antithesis: a pure planned suburb on a new Underground line, on the model set 30 years earlier in Bedford Park. It spawned a host of imitations.

At the end of the first world war, the issue of Garden City versus Garden Suburb became crucial. Raymond Unwin played a key role in the influential Tudor Walters report of 1918 – and then, as chief architect in the Ministry of Health, in its implementation through the Addison Act of 1919 which launched the council housing programme of the interwar years. At that time Howard's own lieutenant, Frederic Osborn, employed as administrator at Letchworth, was calling for a national programme of garden cities. But the call was not heeded: the new houses were built as peripheral suburbs, thus aiding the very suburban sprawl that Howard wanted to avoid. Unwin, so it seemed to many Garden City disciples, had betrayed Howard and rendered his whole campaign nugatory.

Howard did not see it that way. As he told Osborn, if he waited for the government to build garden cities, he would be older than Methusaleh before they started. (That proved slightly less than prophetic: Osborn was 61 when Stevenage was designated in 1946.) Instead, Howard logically proceeded with his pure original vision of garden city construction: in 1920 he bought the nucleus of Welwyn, the second garden city, with money he did not have and then persuaded his friends to bale him out. He lived long enough to move into Welwyn and die there in 1928, a much-loved figure especially popular with children: he looked like Mr Pastry, which must have helped.

Two garden cities in 20 years is no mean achievement for a humble shorthand writer. But – partly perhaps because of the chance of history, partly because the institutional forces were too great, partly because at the end he distrusted governmental action – Howard was not the great architect of 20th century England in general or London in particular. The latter title surely belongs to Frank Pick, a little-known but equally visionary figure who designed the modern London Underground system consciously so as to produce the growth of suburbia – and who then, in the late 1930s, recanted and campaigned for a stop to the whole process.

By that time, Pick was on the winning side. Neville Chamberlain, who had a passionate interest in planning and who had backed Unwin, became Prime Ministr in 1937 and promptly appointed a royal commission on the problem of urban growth. Osborn, as he later confessed in letters to Lewis Mumford, fixed the commission's report from outside: it reported in favour of curbing London's growth and of effective town planning. With equal political skill, in 1945, Osborn persuaded Lewis Silkin – Minister of Planning in Attlee's new government – to back a new towns policy. The New Towns Act received the royal assent on 11 November 1946; Stevenage was designated the same day.

There are final ironies. The new towns were built to a formula designed by that arch-centralist John Reith, and modelled on his BBC: by appointed development corporations financed by Treasury money. It is a formula Howard would doubtless have hated, but at least it built 28 garden cities in 30 years. That was a small fraction of the total growth of urban Britain in that time, but it was something.

In 1975, Lewis Silkin's son, John, introduced the Community Land Act, which at last essentially introduced the land reform Howard had called for. It has been repealed, of course, and the assets of the new towns are being sold off. Prophets, as well as being misunderstood, are without honour in their own country. Meanwhile, Howard's remarkable vision awaits rediscovery.

THE WEBBS

Beatrice Webb 1858–1943
Sidney Webb 1859–1947

Jose Harris

The history of the Webb partnership is perhaps in danger of over-exposure. Over the past decade, the Webbs and their works have been the subject of several mammoth publishing ventures, and for PhD students in search of characters, a visit to the British Library of Political Science has long been an indispensible pilgrimage.

The machiavellian machinations and personal eccentricities of both partners have figured in numerous memoirs. We know that Sidney hid in haystacks to avoid Beatrice's compulsory walks, and that Winston Churchill declined his first cabinet appointment because he "refused to be shut up in a soup kitchen with Mrs Sidney Webb." Among historians there has been much scholarly debate about the Webbs' interpretation of events in which they played a part. Many have questioned their veracity, but few have questioned their historical importance. Their tentacles envelop modern British history, from Bradford to Bloomsbury, from the trade union movement to the City of London, from higher education to the Poor Law, from neo-Darwinist radical imperialism to a romanticised version of stalinism.

Yet, for all this over-exposure, the Webbs remain out of focus. Neither partner has been the subject of a serious intellectual biography. Sidney, in particular, is an enigmatic figure, whose personal gentleness and humility seem oddly out of accord with the pretentiousness and coerciveness of some of his political beliefs. Interpreters of the Webbs have, not surprisingly, concentrated much more closely on their immensely readable letters and on Beatrice's unique diaries, rather than on their vast and dry scholarly works.

Few people realise just how far our consciousness of social history has been shaped by the Webbs, and by their conviction that the foothills of the Poor Law and the shopfloor were just as important as the Himalayan peaks of the constitution. Because neither of the Webbs was a systematic thinker, it is often tempting to dismiss their political writings as hypocritical and confused. It would not be difficult for me to entertain or disgust readers of this article with bizarre demonstrations of the Webbs trying to reconcile elitism with equality, imperialism with nationalism, abolition of differentials with maintenance of incentives, stalinism with quintessential Christianity, sexual puritanism with sexual permissiveness. That the Webbs were muddled and often shifted their ground is undeniable, and nowhere is this more apparent than in their approach to social welfare. I would argue, however, that underlying their frequent shifts of emphasis and strategy was a fairly consistent philosophy of social policy that is of some importance in deciphering the history of welfare statism.

Sidney and Beatrice married in 1892, when Beatrice was still recovering from her passion for Joseph Chamberlain. As many contemporaries maliciously observed, Sidney and Beatrice made an incongruous couple. Beatrice was rich, beautiful, mystical and neurotic, Sidney was plain, pedestrian and poor. She came from the cosmopolitan *haute bourgeoisie*, he from that vein of the London lower middle class that produced *Three Men in a Boat* and Mr Pooter. "I can't help it being Beauty and the Beast," wrote Sidney regretfully, "if only it is not a case of Titania and Bottom."

Intellectually, too, their backgrounds were markedly different. Sidney had been deeply moved by reading *Das Kapital*; but nevertheless, in *Fabian Essays in Socialism*, he had devised a brand of socialism that owed more to Ricardo and Bentham than to Karl Marx. He ascribed economic inequality to the "rent" charged by the different factors of production (land, capital and labour) in proportion to their relative scarcity. The remedy for social evils, he believed, lay in the extension of controls and provision of services by a centralised bureaucratic state. Beatrice, by contrast, was still deeply influenced by the ethic of Social Darwinism, derived from her friend and patron, Herbert Spencer. Though deeply imbued with a spirit of "public service," she had uneasy forebodings of the unintended consequences of well-meaning social actions. "We hear the death groans of the one hundred," she wrote, "we do not hear the life groan of the five hundred until it is too late."

Nevertheless, both the Webbs were resolved, "while there is yet time," to devote themselves and their marriage to the salvation of humanity. This, they believed, could be brought about in two ways. First, by the discovery of an empirically-based "science of society," which would make possible rational diagnosis of social problems; and, secondly, by the reconstruction of British social institutions to meet what they saw as the functional imperatives of modern industrial life.

These two tasks they believed to be intimately bound up with each other, thus locking themselves into the first of the great logical contradictions that beset their intellectual careers. When assessing the Webbs as social researchers, it must be remembered that every fact they ever collected was designed to fulfil two mutually exclusive functions: to prove that facts "spoke for themselves," without reference to theory, *and* to prove that history was moving inexorably in a certain predetermined way.

The Webbs' work as practical reformers was greatly helped by Beatrice's private income (about £1,500 a year in the 1900s, equivalent to the salary of the head of a civil service department or three times that of the average solicitor in private practice; 20 times the wage of a skilled working man). This enabled Sidney to retire from his post in the Colonial Office and devote himself exclusively to politics and private research.

The Webbs' career in politics may be seen as falling into four distinct though overlapping phases. First, in the early 1890s, their hopes were pinned on "Progressivism." They hoped that this would forge a common ethic of collectivism among trade unionists, state socialists and left-wing Gladstonian Liberals.

When Progressivism petered out (or rather, failed to advance along the lines prescribed by Fabians), they turned their attention to permeating the minds of politicians of all persuasions – convincing themselves that the onward march of socialism was part of an irresistible evolutionary process common to all groups in society. It was during this second period (late 1890s to late 1900s) that the Webbs served mutton chops in their salon at Grosvenor Road, weekended in country houses with cabinet ministers, espoused the cause of "national efficiency," and earned their reputation as the high-minded but unscrupulous manipulators lampooned by H. G. Wells in *The New Machiavelli*.

The failure of their Poor Law campaign in the late 1900s led to disenchantment with "permeation," and persuaded them that socialism could only come about through a party based on the organised working class. Hence the third phase – their active commitment to the Labour Party after 1912. Within the party they fought a long-drawn-out battle to save its soul from anarcho-syndicalism, drafted detailed plans for the functionalist reconstruction of government, and devised an ideal socialist constitution designed to re-vamp British democracy at all levels from parliament to village street. Sidney himself served as a cabinet minister in the minority Labour governments of 1924 and 1929. (He was created Baron Passfield in 1929, Beatrice remaining plain Mrs Webb.)

But Labour, like other parties, proved curiously resistant to Webbian visions of social reconstruction. So, in 1932, there came their fourth and final political phase, when they visited the Soviet Union. The result was not so much conversion as revelation – the revelation that all the services, principles and policies that they had long been pressing for were already in existence in Russia, organised by cadres of party officials motivated by samurai-like efficiency and early Christian dedication. As Margaret Cole remarked, the Webbs in Stalin's Russia beheld "Fabian socialism in action" – a comment that says little for their powers of empirical observation, but tells us a great deal about their social and political ideas.

The differing concerns of the four stages of the Webbs' political career were, to a certain extent, mirrored by their ideas on social policy. In their earliest phase, their approach to social questions was closely linked to their interest in municipal socialism and trade unionism. Sidney was elected to the London County Council in 1892. As chairman of the council's Technical Education Board, he was responsible for London's impressive development of "polytechnic" schools, and for creating a scholarship ladder for working class children up to the level of university. With other Fabian councillors he strongly supported the Progressive majority's policy of extending public services, and acting as a model employer to the council's own employees. In 1894 he was responsible for drafting the Minority Report of the Royal Commission on Labour – a document that had strong "social welfare," as well as industrial implications, since it recommended statutory enforcement of minimum wages and health conditions for workers too weak to protect themselves by collective bargaining.

In 1896 the Webbs first formulated their famous doctrine of the "National Minimum." It is interesting to note that this doctrine (often thought of as one of the guiding principles of the welfare state) was originally rooted in the Webbs' studies of trade unionism, rather than of social administration. It was based on the principle that the "common rule" of minimum wages and conditions achieved by the most powerful unions should be extended by a mixture of state enforcement and collective bargaining to the whole community.

Many of the Webbs' writings make it clear that this conception of parallel action by state and trade unions to achieve an integrated twofold goal of "social" and "industrial" welfare never vanished from their thought. But nevertheless, around the turn of the century, the Webbs were estranged from the trade union movement. They were only partially sympathetic to the union case on Taff Vale. They were disappointed with the lack of "state-conscious idealism" among trade union leaders, and their general indifference to the socialistic benefits of South African imperialism. Consequently, trade unionism receded from the forefront of their thinking, and was replaced by bureaucratic reform and the setting-up of the "housekeeping state." It was now that they first began to formulate their ideal model of how central and local services should be reformed – a model that is difficult to describe accurately without resort to the leaden and robot-like prose with which the Webbs themselves habitually discussed administrative questions.

They proposed that, at central level, government offices which had grown up historically and higgledy-piggledy should be replaced by specialist departments devoted to a single function – such as Education, Employment, Housing, Agriculture, Health. And at local level, control of all services should be concentrated in the hands of specialist committees of county councils – thus doing away with the tangle of ad-hoc local authorities, such as school boards and Poor Law guardians that had grown up piecemeal during the course of the 19th century.

The Webbs' philosophy of functionalist social administration first found expression in the battle over control of secondary education in the early 1900s. In this they strongly supported the policy of their friend, Arthur Balfour, in concentrating educational provision under a centralised Board of Education, and in transferring local control from directly-elected school boards to committees of county councils. The principle behind this change – which was seen at the time as a victory for "experts" over amateurs and parents – was one which the Webbs wholeheartedly approved.

The functionalist philosophy came much more strongly to the fore, however, in the contest over the Royal Commission on the Poor Laws that was fought out between 1905 and 1909. Beatrice was appointed a member of the commission in 1905, and rapidly found herself locked in combat with her fellow-members, the majority of whom were either civil servants or representatives of "organised charity." With Sidney's support, she disdained the research carried out by the other commissioners, mounted her own detailed inquiry into Poor Law problems, and eventually produced her own massive minority report – a document that is often seen as the Magna Carta of the British welfare state.

In fact, like the Magna Carta, the Webbs' minority report contained almost the exact opposite of what popular mythology supposed. In the 1920s, the Webbs liked to portray their brainchild as a classic of democratic socialism. In reality, it was a classic of administrative functionalism and professionalisation. The scope of the minority report and the Webbs' disagreements with the majority cannot be considered in detail here, but the most important points at issue may be summarised as follows.

Both reports agreed that the 1834 Poor Law had irrevocably broken down, and both agreed that boards of guardians should be abolished;

but they disagreed about what should take their place. The Webbs proposed that specialist central departments and specialist local committees should manage all social services on the lines already laid down by the Education Act, 1902. In other words, the Board of Education and local education committees should be joined by parallel ministries and county council committees, dealing with health, employment and housing and so on. The majority agreed in seeing the county council as the focal point of future social administration, but they proposed a single committee to deal with all problems of social dependancy – a policy which they defended in terms rather similar to that of the Seebohm report of 1968 (namely that most social problems were "family" problems rather than areas of clearly-defined specialisation).

The two reports also disagreed about who was to run the new services. The minority envisaged the employment of a new profession of trained administrators and social workers; the majority envisaged that charitable volunteers would continue to play a major role for a long time to come. The majority thought that the scope of the new services would be largely confined to those unable to help themselves through voluntary societies, whereas the minority argued that modern social systems required social services on a "universal" basis (though it is important to note that by this term they did not mean "universal" in the Beveridge sense, but services "for the whole of the working class, with charge and recovery from those able to pay").

Perhaps the most substantial difference in the proposals of the two reports lay, however, in their policies for unemployment. The majority proposed the setting up of voluntary labour exchanges and the tentative introduction of state-subsidised unemployment insurance. The minority, by contrast, proposed compulsory labour exchanges and far-reaching state regulation of all aspects of employment. Hiring and firing except through exchanges would become illegal. Redundant workers would be compulsorily retrained in state workshops and labour colonies. The unemployable and the workshy would be subject to penal detention. The national market for labour would be managed "like a gigantic drainage system," by a central department of state. In addition, aggregate demand would be regulated and cyclical unemployment minimised by adjustments in the bank rate and concentration of government expenditure into periods of depression.

The Webbs never wavered in the view that their minority report contained the ideal blueprint for the social services of a modern industrial state. What did waver was their conviction that their proposals were likely to be adopted. In the years before the first world war, they organised a nationwide campaign for the break-up of the Poor

Law. Almost certainly, this was of much significance in mobilising grassroots support for the Labour Party at that time.

In the euphoric postwar reconstruction period, the Webbs were confident that their vision of the social order was on the brink of implementation. Yet Labour, once in office, showed no more enthusiasm for state regulation of the labour market than Liberals or Conservatives. Throughout the 1920s, the Webbs' solution for unemployment was almost totally ignored in Labour circles – doubtless because any attempt to enact its more coercive elements, or even to adopt them as Labour policy, would have instantly alienated the trade unions and individual working men. The Webbs blamed the neglect of their ideas on capitalist selfishness and "plutocratic over-confidence," but in fact their main rejection came from socialists more liberally minded than themselves. In the event, the politician who gained most from the Webbs was Neville Chamberlain. In 1929, he carried through the administrative part of their Poor Law reforms, while carefully ignoring their economic and social policies.

The Webbs have often been seen as political trimmers and pragmatists with no coherent objectives beyond the leaden ideals of "permeation" and "gradualness." This view seems to me profoundly incorrect. From a very early stage the Webbs had a clear idea of the kind of society they wanted, and a deep conviction that history was bringing it about. All that varied was their conception of how fast history was moving, and of the tactics they should use to help it on its way.

The Webbs' vision of the future was perhaps most succinctly spelt out in Sidney's chapter on "Social movements" for the *Cambridge Modern History*, written in 1908. There he set out his conviction that society was advancing, not merely in Britain but globally, along five parallel lines: collective ownership of capital, municipal provision of social services, state regulation of residual private property, redistributive taxation to remove remaining inequalities, and a national minimum to help those unable to help themselves.

The rationale behind this fivefold progress Sidney defined as the "application of the lessons which political economy has learnt from biology and from Darwinism, as a fundamental necessity of national existence." The beneficiaries of this movement were not the individual members of society, not even the weak and helpless, but the corporate group. The aim of the national minimum was to confer education, sanitation, leisure and subsistence on every citizen, " whether he likes it or not." The process involved the gradual elimination of families and other social groupings that stood between the citizen and the wider community. Unlike the organic structures envisaged by conservative theorists, the organic structures of modern collectivism would contain only "the individual human being whether man or woman, infant or adult . . . as the unit of the social order." All that was needed to complete the process, wrote Beatrice, was the development of a "genuinely state-conscious collective mind and the machinery to carry this will into effect."

This is not the place for a general discussion of the Webbs' political philosophy. But I will conclude with a few comments on their ideas and attitudes in so far as these relate to their theory of the welfare state.

One thing that is clear from many of their writings is that the Webbs did not believe in moral freedom in the normal English usage of that term. They did not think it possible for an individual or groups of individuals to have convictions at odds with those of the whole community and be right. Sidney often referred to himself as applying to the social sphere the same kind of reasoning about the "general will" that Rousseau applied to the political sphere: this comparison seems to me correct. "This false metaphysical idea of rights," bemoaned Beatrice, "working its wicked way in our political life."

A second point is that the Webbs' reputation as Gradgrind British empiricists seems to me totally false. Gradgrinds they may have been, but empiricists they were not. Indeed, their whole philosophy might be said to have been rooted in a profound contempt for facts, except in so far as these could be used to batter unbelievers into submission.

A third point is that their analysis of society took almost no account of the realities of economic or political power. They failed to build into their critique of capitalism any prediction that capitalists might resist radical redistributional change. When capitalists did so, the Webbs were absurdly surprised and confounded. Similarly, they were naively indifferent to the fact that concentrated state power could be used in many different ways. The Webbian state was always a beast of burden, never a beast of prey. Hence their bewilderment in the whirlwind of the 1930s.

A further point that comes out very clearly from the Webb correspondence is that both partners were profoundly ill at ease in an atmosphere of diversity and conflict. This may seem an odd comment, in view of the zeal with which time and again the Webbs hurled themselves into public battles. But they did so in the conviction that all rational people would eventually come round to their point of view.

"Sidney," observed Bernard Shaw, "conceives himself a commonplace sensible Englishman, living in a world of just such commonplace Englishmen . . . everything must yield to commonsense in such a world." When, however, it became ever more clear that the world was not yielding, the Webbs grew baffled and dispirited. Their letters of the 1920s, particularly those of Beatrice, were increasingly oppressed by the moral, political and sexual anarchy that seemed to engulf the world. This was another reason for the charm of stalinism. There was no room in the Webb vision for plurality of ends.

Because the Webbs always insisted on writing about social policy in such grandiose schematic terms, these flaws in their wider outlook cannot be lightly dismissed. Unfortunately, such faults tend to obscure many of the positive, if more humdrum, contributions that the Webbs made to social policy issues – such as their active support for technical education, their very constructive emphasis on preventive and community medicine, and their (at the time highly original) proposals for countermanding cyclical unemployment.

There is one important question on which I think the Webbs were probably right, and that is that unemployment cannot be cured in advanced economies, either capitalist or socialist, without some curtailment of personal freedom. The Webbs faced this issue much more straightly than most writers on unemployment problems are prepared to do. They would have defended their position by claiming that personal freedom was illusory, and that mass security of employment was in any case worth the price.

R.L. MORANT
1863–1920

Harry Judge

On the morning of Boxing Day, 1898, a relatively junior civil servant let himself into his office at 43 Parliament Street. Robert Morant, never orthodox in his methods, had chosen that festive day for a discreet meeting with a London County Council official. His purpose was to draw attention to material that could be used by the LCC to overturn the prevailing policy of his own superiors. The effects of Morant's calculated indiscretions included the creation of the national system of education as we know it, and his own surprising elevation into the place of the Permanent Secretary against whom he had so effectively plotted.

Morant's career to date had been a shade exotic. Born into an Evangelical household in Hampstead and battling against severe financial difficulties, he had made his way through Winchester to read classics and theology at New College, Oxford. Growing doubts about Christianity deflected him from the clerical career on which he had set his mind, into prep school teaching and years as tutor to the royal princes of Siam. His sense of grand purpose, nourished by Florence Nightingale, was applied to the systematic improvement of education in Siam. All that was swept away by the political crisis of 1893, and the substitution in Bangkok of French for English influence.

A discouraged Morant came home in search of work, and took up residence in the East End of London at Toynbee Hall, moving into the industrious circle of Sidney and Beatrice Webb. In 1895, the civil servant, Michael Sadler, took him on as his assistant in the Education Office and both now became closely involved in the research and preparation underlying the act of 1899, which created one central body in Whitehall – the Board of Education – to superintend all the unrelated parts of educational provision in Britain.

When the Board was created, both Sadler and Morant became civil servants there. Much work was needed to make its authority effective. Any such efforts would be frustrated – or so Morant came to think – unless order and system could now be introduced into the local arrangements for the management of education. This was the congenial doctrine preached by Sidney Webb, and published by him in the short and lucid pamphlet, *The Education Muddle and the Way Out*. The muddle was one of competing authorities (local and national), incoherent policies (where they existed at all), legal doubts, insufficient provision and waste.

Parliament had in the 19th century been unwilling to establish a national system of education. The concept was perceived as despotic and the cost as unacceptable. Education was properly the business of private enterprise and charitable effort, notably by the churches. The churches made heroic efforts to meet such needs, and from the 1830s onwards received annual government grants to assist them.

Nevertheless, the Anglican monopoly in many parts of the country-side was deeply resented, and the rapid growth of towns outpaced whatever voluntary effort could be stimulated. Eventually, in Forster's Education Act of 1870, local school boards were established to provide a framework of public elementary schools supported by rates and government grants. A dual system had been absentmindedly created in elementary education. In many places the parson and the school board glowered at one another, and fought for pupils and resources.

What charitable effort, supplemented belatedly by state support, had achieved in elementary education was largely left to private enterprise in secondary schooling. But the spectre of foreign competition and technological obsolescence – never far distant from the uneasy English conscience – persuaded parliament in the 1880s into making money available for technical and scientific education, and allowing the county councils and county boroughs to raise more through the rates for the same purpose. These funds were available as grants to be paid to support particular courses in existing schools.

The position was anomalous. Central and local government could apply funds to educational purposes but could not by law maintain schools. School boards could by law maintain schools within the elementary category. Inevitably these boards were virtuously tempted to meet rising educational demand by applying their own resources, and such grants as they could secure, to developing courses in their schools beyond the elementary level.

Morant's Permanent Secretary at the Board of Education, Sir George Kekewich, combined an unveiled contempt for the politicians who were his constitutional masters with an affection for the school boards. Throughout the 1890s he encouraged the local school boards to develop the Higher Grade school – charging low fees, disturbing the (relatively few) established grammar schools by the threat of subsidised competition, and providing an alternative style of curriculum to the more traditional offerings of those self-consciously academic establishments.

It is, I believe, an error to suppose that Morant objected in principle to alternative forms of (almost) secondary education. What he disliked was their dubiously legal sponsorship by the school boards, the lack of coherence in the pattern that was rapidly developing, and the absence of coordination between the local authorities, established by the Local Government Act of 1888, and the elementary education authorities established 18 years before that.

Morant could not have engineered the Education Act of 1902 – and that is precisely what he did – without some powerful allies. Dramatic events followed the meeting on Boxing Day, 1898. Morant drew the attention of his LCC allies to a passage in a report he had written on education in Switzerland, pointing out that school boards were exceeding their powers in providing education other than elementary.

The LCC's powerful Technical Education Board, of which Webb had been chairman, provoked a challenge to the London School Board. Cockerton, the local auditor, ruled that the school board had indeed no right to spend the ratepayer's money on anything other than the purposes specified by the 1870 act. The cat was now out of the bag. Subsequent appeals by the school board confirmed the correctness of Cockerton's ruling.

Morant saw his opportunity: which, given that he created it, is hardly surprising. Existing practice had been declared illegal, and no government could refuse to act. Morant moved quickly, making himself indispensable to Sir John Gorst, the minister in the Conservative government. A quiet luncheon party was also arranged by Edward Talbot, bishop of Rochester and formerly warden of Keble, for Morant to meet Balfour – already Leader of the House of Commons and shortly to succeed his uncle, the Earl of Salisbury, as Prime Minister.

Although Balfour had to leave over coffee, a great impression had been made. Morant was invited to let Balfour have a draft of a bill. Gorst joined Sadler and Kekewich in the company of those whom Morant had by-passed. After the second reading of the bill, Morant became full-time assistant to Balfour. In 1902, Kekewich was asked to relinquish the Permanent Secretaryship in order to make way for someone who would be "a glutton for work." That proved to be Morant.

Balfour's act, even more than R.A. Butler's successor in 1944, provided the contemporary framework for the educational system of this country. Adjustments have, of course, been made – not least in Fisher's Act of 1918 – to the balance of relationships between central and local government. Indeed, at this moment, that relationship is under scrutiny and strain. It remains unlikely, at least in this century, that the local authorities as defined in 1902 will lose their educational responsibility.

Morant made full use of the religious question to provide the "head of steam" for the reform to which he had committed himself. Without the religious "problem," it is doubtful whether, even against the background of the Cockerton affair, the Conservative Party could have been mobilised by Balfour to take the giant step of 1902.

For the Church of England especially, the problem in the 1890s was essentially financial. The voluntary societies looked anxiously at what seemed to them the extravagance of the school boards in enlarging their premises, improving the pay of their teachers, extending the curriculum beyond the limits of the elementary codes – all this with the encouragement of the officials in Whitehall. The resources for church schools were straitened, and the schools themselves at breaking point.

Any attempt to increase central government grants – or, even worse, to introduce the novelty of local government grants – could be relied upon to inflame opposition. But, at a time when half the children at school were in voluntary schools, the problem could not be ignored. The first obstacle to overcome was the opposition of Balfour's own political allies, the Liberal Unionists. Morant was despatched to Birmingham to persuade the formidable Joe Chamberlain that there was only one way forward. He regarded his success on that mission as the greatest victory of his life.

The Liberal opposition, however, took a very different view and filled its sails with the gale of indignation that raged against Rome (and indeed Canterbury) on the rates. Lloyd George took full advantage of the occasion to display his passion and his rhetoric, and established his reputation as a parliamentarian. In Wales there were extensive pockets of resistance and a boycott of rates. Such extreme opposition (as Balfour predicted) fizzled out, but the unpopularity of this necessary part of the measure contributed to the massive defeat of Balfour's party in the general election of 1906.

The victorious Liberal Party honoured its promise to abolish state support for the voluntary schools by introducing a bill, but the Lords demolished it – so adding to that catalogue of offences which was to lead to their emasculation in 1911. By then tempers had cooled, and the settlement of 1902 became an (apparently) permanent part of English educational and political life. At all events, Churchill (remembering the troubles of the early century) required Butler, when he was drafting the 1944 act, to do nothing to disturb the precarious balance established in 1902. Massive financial support for denominational schools within a framework of local provision became as much a part of the accepted world as the dominance of the local education authority.

The department which Morant inherited as Permanent Secretary in 1902 had been formally constituted as the Board of Education in 1899 (to become the Ministry of Education in 1944, and the Department of Education and Science in 1964). Morant relished the work of giving detailed shape to the new department. He established four branches with clearly defined functions – Elementary, Secondary, Technical, and Special Inquiries and Reports – and ensured that the organisation of Her Majesty's Inspectorate coincided with and served the needs of those branches. Much as he respected inspectors, and enjoyed working with them, he would have found offensive the assertion of independence which is now often made on their behalf.

Morant is best, although not always accurately, remembered for the ways in which he used the authority of the Board to consolidate the establishment of that most English of institutions – the maintained secondary grammar school. The sinister version of his influence is that he issued regulations governing the payment of grants related to the nature of the curriculum in such a way as to stifle the promising growth of alternative forms of secondary education. He is represented as the enemy of vocationalism and modernism – the unimaginative and determined Wykehamist who imposed on the country secondary schools modelled on the ancient grammar schools and the successful public schools.

The truth is a little different. The regulations of 1904 did indeed require that three and a half hours each week should be devoted to a foreign language, six hours if two languages were taught, and that an explanation would be required if Latin were *not* one of those two languages. But, as Olive Banks has shown, such a requirement was widely welcomed as a careful attempt to reduce the imbalance that had crept into the curriculum – a distortion caused by the allocation of grants in the 1890s for the teaching of useful and modern subjects. Moreover, the same regulations required seven and a half hours for mathematics and science (including practical work), and detailed requirements were in any case shortly withdrawn.

Morant may indeed have been well-disposed towards a more traditional grammar school curriculum, but it was not necessary to impose it upon a reluctant public, Morant presided over a department which in 1910 had 92 senior staff members, of whom 58 had been educated at Oxford (36 of them in Greats) and 23 at Cambridge (14 in Classics). Their vision of the curriculum was not a revolutionary one.

Morant and Balfour seem indeed to have been surprised by the pressure coming from local education authorities to establish grammar schools, reflecting (not for the last time) the preference of parents for forms of curriculum and education which gave access to higher education and the more highly esteemed professions. There was, moreover, an urgent need for teachers with the background of what was conventionally and not improperly regarded as a good general education.

There is no need to dress Morant in the clothes of an early egalitarian, or even of an R.H. Tawney. His passion was for order and good government, and for the development of a relatively restricted system of secondary education of high quality. There was in his temperament more than a touch of arrogance, and his enemies in the educational world were multiplying.

Although Morant was, in the terms which Balfour would have understood, a conservative, he remained a highly professional civil servant, and made the necessary adjustments when the Liberals came to power in 1905. He may not have taken pleasure in the attacks upon the "undemocratic spirit" of the Board, but he drafted the free place regulations of 1907 with his usual care.

These regulations, in effect, inverted existing policy. Whereas, since 1903, secondary schools could not normally receive grants unless they kept free (or scholarship) places to a limit of 25 per cent, that maximum would hereafter be a minimum. The 11-plus had been established, whatever the private views of Morant. He did, however, clearly recognise that a change of this order would require changes in the curriculum, and did his best to encourage them.

His critics found their opportunity for revenge in 1911. There was an outcry about an HMI report (intended only for restricted circulation) which made injudicious references to the lack of culture and education among elementary school teachers. The outcry was orchestrated by the National Union of Teachers, who were also affronted by the Permanent Secretary's filibustering opposition to the introduction of a Teacher's Register, and Morant was sacrificed.

His fall was, however, far from catastrophic and his achievement in education survived intact. Lloyd George, who had noticed his quality in 1902, invited Morant to preside over the introduction of his new national insurance scheme. The challenge to create a new department where none existed was relished by Morant and the group of able administrators he gathered around him. He had already initiated a school medical service, freely acknowledging his debt to the influence of Margaret MacMillan and the partnership with George Newman, and the new work was congenial.

Again, his vision was one of creating a unitary Ministry of Health, comparable with Education, and similarly articulated with local provision. He resisted the pretensions of the British Medical Association with the same determination as he had shown towards the NUT, refusing to allow sectional interests to stand in the way of what he perceived as good social policy and sound administrative practice. He worked closely with Christopher Addison, the Minister of Reconstruction, and was rewarded not only by seeing the Ministry of Health created in 1919 but also by becoming its first Permanent Secretary. At the age of 56, he was ready to create a new department of state.

It is, however, for his work in education that he will be principally remembered – as the architect of a new department, as the friend (if one were needed) of the secondary grammar school, as the negotiator of an elaborate partnership with the churches, as the first man in central government to stress the centrality of health and child welfare among public commitments in education, as the champion of the new responsibilities of the local education authorities. All but one of those achievements has left a powerful impression upon the educational system of the welfare state. Even the apparent exception (the grammar school) dominated English educational history for the next 60 years, and directly influenced the manner in which comprehensive secondary schooling is now developing.

It would be absurd to argue that none of these things would have happened without Morant, or could have happened if the time had not been ripe, if the Conservatives had been out of power, if the churches had not themselves desperately needed a settlement, or if the campaign against the school boards had not already been vigorous. But much was due to "that magnificent hustler," as Christopher Addison gratefully dubbed him. His successor, Sir Amherst Selby-Bigge, more chastely described his methods as "unorthodox." Sadler and Kekewich had more bitter things to say.

Late in February 1920 he told the inaugural meeting of the Society of Civil Servants: "I always regard men and women who work at all seriously at things as falling into two classes roughly – those who leave absolutely no stone unturned to make the things they are at a success and" (here he paused and with a smile continued) "those who turn just enough stones to make it just about do."

He died on 13 March in the same year.

LLOYD GEORGE
1863–1945

John Grigg

Probably no man did more towards establishing the foundations of a welfare state in Britain than David Lloyd George. Many would describe him, quite simply, as the creator of our welfare state. But does he really deserve the title and, if so, did he really know what he was doing? Was he a genuine social reformer – a genuine believer in the use of state power to improve the condition of the people – or was he merely a brilliant opportunist and demagogue, whose name happens to be associated with measures for which others deserve more of the credit?

Lloyd George was, of course, quintessentially a politician. He was neither an economist nor a political scientist, and in general had very little taste or time for abstract thought. His concern was always for the concrete and the practical, and in some ways his motto might have been: "I do not ask to see the distant scene; one step enough for me." Yet this could be very misleading if it were taken to mean that he had no aims beyond the ground immediately ahead of him. On the contrary, his approach to politics was exceptionally imaginative. But his imagination did not make him unrealistic, or lead him into ideological formulations which might have distracted him from the tasks in hand, and would certainly have restricted his freedom to manoeuvre and compromise. It would be true to say that he had a broad *sense* of the future, rather than a precise *vision* of it.

His childhood in North Wales was austere and frugal, without being exactly poor. Culturally he belonged to a self-conscious elite – the Welsh-speaking, chapel-going, professional elite, which was conveniently coming into its own at the time of his youth. Resentment of the hereditary rich (especially landlords) came, therefore, more naturally to someone of his background than sympathy with the poor – though poverty, together with the sickness and other evils that attended it, did in fact profoundly disgust and horrify him.

Speaking even before his first election to parliament at the early age of 27, he said that familiar Welsh causes such as Disestablishment and local option only touched the fringes "of the vast social question which must be dealt with in the near future." A holy war, he said, had been proclaimed against man's inhumanity to man. Thus he was committed, at the outset of his career, to social reform unlimited, though also undefined. And he wrote in an article at about the same time that it was "an odd fact about all reforms that they have been brought about by persons outside the sufferers themselves." He was to be a case in point, and he knew it, though of course he made good rhetorical use of his relatively humble origins.

During his 15 years as a backbencher – from 1890 to 1905 – he devoted most of his time to just the sort of tribal and sectarian issues that he had himself described as peripheral to the social question. (The only major exception was his opposition to the Boer war, which had the important effect of making him a household name.) He had not forgotten social reform, but knew that before he could achieve anything big he had first to attain power; and that to attain power he had to use all the leverage that Wales and Nonconformity could give him as a Welsh Liberal politician. Had he neglected his base, he might not have been such a strong candidate for high office when the Liberals returned to power. As it was, he stepped straight into the Campbell-Bannerman cabinet as President of the Board of Trade.

Not long before, he had reasserted his social reforming faith in a speech (at Newcastle, in April 1903) which anticipated his 1909 budget and his Land Campaign of 1913–14. But while he was at the Board of Trade, he concentrated on showing that he could run a department, and that he could be conciliatory as well as challenging. His principal measures were virtually agreed with the opposition, and his handling of the railway dispute in 1907 was widely acclaimed. But he still made radical speeches at weekends, to remind people that he had not fundamentally changed. In one (at Penrhyndeudraeth, in September 1906) he said: "There is more wealth per head of the population here than in any other land in the world. Shame upon rich Britain that she should tolerate so much poverty among her people! . . . What is wanted is fairer distribution."

When, in April 1908, Asquith succeeded Campbell-Bannerman as Prime Minister, and Lloyd George took Asquith's place as Chancellor of the Exchequer, the opportunity came to match words with deeds. But Lloyd George did not arrive at the Treasury with any thought-out scheme of reform. Pragmatist that he was, he began to apply his mind to the subject in detail only when he was in a position to get things done, and when he knew that the time was ripe.

His first big achievement was the Old Age Pensions Act, which became law in August 1908. The principle of old age pensions was reaffirmed by Asquith in the budget for that year (which he introduced after becoming Prime Minister), but it fell to Lloyd George to carry out the legislation. As a result, he obtained most of the credit and the pension was popularly known, for a time, as the "Lloyd George." This was only fair, because – unlike Asquith and most of his other cabinet colleagues – he had been seriously committed to old age pensions for some years, and had served on a House of Commons select committee on the matter in 1899. Moreover, he piloted the measure through parliament with great skill, showing all the firmness and flexibility which together made him such an effective reformer under democratic conditions.

The British system of old age pensions, as established by Lloyd George's act, followed the New Zealand rather than the German model, in that it was non-contributory and therefore financed out of general taxation. In its original form the scheme provided for a pension of 5 shillings (25p) a week for all individuals over 70, and 7s 6d (37½p) a week for couples. But they had to have incomes of less than £26 a week (or £39 in the case of couples), and apart from those with higher incomes there were a few other disqualified categories, such as criminals, lunatics and loafers. In committee, Lloyd George accepted two important amendments to the scheme. The abrupt cut-off at £26 was replaced by a sliding-scale between incomes of £21 and £31 10 shillings (£31.50p), and the lower rate of pension for couples was cancelled in favour of the full rate for each partner.

In his second reading speech on the bill, Lloyd George stressed that it was only a "first step," and promised further measures to tackle the "problems of the sick, of the infirm, of the men who cannot find a means of earning a livelihood . . . problems which the state has neglected too long." The following year he introduced the great budget which provided the funds for such an expansion of state activity.

It should be said at this point that Lloyd George was by no means a wholehearted rebel against Victorian notions of sound finance. Though he was determined that the state should concern itself more with promoting the welfare of citizens, he was far from believing that a Chancellor of the Exchequer had no obligation to balance the books or to look for economies. Personally, he was reckless about money, acting as a rule on the assumption that he had plenty of it, but at the same time his mind was haunted by the doctrine of thrift which emanated from his home environment.

This schizophrenia was reflected in his attitude towards public finance; and as he began to prepare for his 1909 budget he hoped, at first, to be able to make the necessary funds available for social reform by securing cuts elsewhere, more especially in expenditure on the armed forces. But this did not prove possible, and he was therefore compelled to meet an estimated deficit of £16½ million largely by increased taxation.

The scope of the 1909 budget was unprecedented. As a leading Unionist, Austen Chamberlain, said in his immediate reaction to it, Lloyd George had "sketched a budget not for the year only, but for a series of years," and with it a legislative programme "trenching upon the province of almost every one of his colleagues." Lloyd George himself said that it was "a war budget . . . for raising money to wage inplacable warfare against poverty and squalidness." The money raised would go not only towards paying for old age pensions but also, he said, "to make some further provision for the sick, for the invalided, for widows and orphans," and "to deal on a comprehensive scale with the problem of unemployment." There was also provision, in the budget, for children's allowances to parents with incomes of under £500 a year.

The burden of new taxation was truly progressive, in that it bore most heavily upon the rich, who were still, at that date, grossly undertaxed. Apart from increased duties on tobacco and spirits, most of the new indirect taxation was on luxuries, as for instance motor vehicles and petrol – taxed for the first time as the luxuries they then were. But, above all, Lloyd George shifted the tax burden appreciably from indirect to direct. Whereas the proportions had been about equal when he took office, by 1914 indirect taxes represented less than 40 per cent of the total. Moreover, he made sure that a preponderant share of the direct taxation was paid by those best able to pay.

The graduation of income tax on the whole benefited the middle class, while demanding more of the rich, who were further hit by Lloyd George's new super-tax, brought in in 1909 and put on a graduated basis in 1914. Death duties, also, were substantially increased (though even so they only reached, by 1914, a top rate of 20 per cent on estates in excess of £1 million). The controversial land taxes were of very small account in themselves, but important for the valuation of land that they were intended to involve.

Because of the constitutional conflict between Lords and Commons that the 1909 budget provoked, it was not until April 1910 that it was passed into law. Meanwhile, Lloyd George had been starting to plan the large extension of state-sponsored welfare which the budget was designed to facilitate. His chief partner in this work was Winston Churchill, his successor at the Board of Trade, and in February 1910 Churchill's system of labour exchanges came into operation. This was a prelude to the unemployment insurance which formed part II of Lloyd George's National Insurance Bill in 1911.

The scheme was compulsory, but limited to trades in which

unemployment was cyclical rather than chronic, such as shipbuilding, mechanical engineering and the construction industry. Contributions were to be made by employers, employees and the Exchequer, and the state further undertook to provide up to £3 million in case the insurance fund could not meet all the demands on it. The rate of benefit was fixed at 7 shillings (35p) per week for a maximum of 15 weeks within any twelve-month period.* (After the first world war the scale of the problem had become so much vaster that Lloyd George's coalition government had to discard the insurance principle in favour of means-tested unemployment relief, though later, during the second world war, the principle was resurrected – on paper – in the Beveridge scheme).

Part I of Lloyd George's National Insurance Bill, for which he took the sole responsibility, was designed to provide a universal compulsory system of health insurance, including funeral benefit and provision for widows and orphans (though these had to be dropped under pressure from the industrial insurance "combine"). Lloyd George's scheme differed from the Bismarckian system in Germany – which he had taken the trouble to study at first hand during the summer of 1908 – above all in that it excluded old age pensions (which, as we have seen, were made non-contributory), and that it involved a much larger contribution from the state.

Lloyd George's original idea was to administer the scheme through the friendly societies, but he soon ran into trouble with the "combine." He had to modify his scheme so as to bring industrial insurance, as well, into the process of administration. Far worse, however, was the trouble that he encountered with the doctors, which was not finally resolved until the scheme came into operation, with the first payment of benefits, in January 1913. In the end the British Medical Association overbid its hand, and Lloyd George was able to call its bluff. But earlier he had made concessions to the doctors which had the very desirable effect of giving better prospects to young recruits to the profession, and of putting up the value of practices, not least in working class areas. Bernard Shaw wrote in 1911 (in the preface to *The Doctor's Dilemma*): "Nothing is more dangerous than a poor doctor." Beyond question, Lloyd George's health insurance scheme, as amended, decisively improved the pay and status of ordinary doctors, in the process ensuring that they would in future give better service to ordinary people.

The scheme made health insurance compulsory for all regularly employed workers over the age of 16, and with incomes below the level

* According to Treasury figures, £1 in 1911 was worth £32.11 in today's (1984) money.

of income tax liability; also for all manual workers, whatever their income. Contributions were to be at the rate of fourpence (about 1½p) a week from a man (threepence for a woman); threepence a week from the employer; and twopence a week from the state. The contributions therefore added up to ninepence a week, with the male employee paying only fourpence. Hence Lloyd George's famous phrase, "ninepence for fourpence" – which rather backfired on him, however, because workers of the type not accustomed to putting money aside knew all too well that fourpence a week was being deducted from their wages, but felt that the ninepence was a somewhat insubstantial entity, since it was not immediately available.

In fact, the benefits were quite substantial in relation to the money values of the time. Sick pay was at the rate of 10 shillings (50p) a week for men, and 7s 6d (37½p) a week for women, from the fourth day of illness, for a period of 13 weeks. For the next 13 weeks the sick person, of either sex, would receive 5 shillings (25p) a week, and thereafter 5 shillings a week disability benefit, which might continue indefinitely. There was also medical benefit – the right to attention from a GP, with the appropriate treatment and medicines, and the more specific right to treatment for tuberculosis in a sanatorium. Finally, there was maternity benefit of 30 shillings (£1.50), paid direct to the insured man's wife; or of £3 if both husband and wife were insured.

The scheme was a great blessing to the majority of the British people and above all to the wives and children of those workers who, unlike the "aristocrats of labour," had previously failed to insure themselves. Two clear indications of its success are that the number of men and women receiving Poor Law relief, which had been rising steadily since the 1880s, began to decline after 1912; and that, after the scheme came into operation, many fewer people attended hospitals as out-patients, while many more were admitted to hospital for the treatment of serious illness.

Without Lloyd George's unique combination of dynamism, resourcefulness and adaptability it is most unlikely that the scheme would have been carried through. Though he had many talented and devoted helpers, the credit for what was achieved is due overwhelmingly to him. He did not, however, regard it as an end in itself, nor was he wedded to insurance as a principle. In March 1911 he wrote to his private secretary, R.G. Hawtrey: "Insurance necessarily temporary expedient. At no distant date hope state will acknowledge full responsibility in the matter of making provision for sickness, breakdown and unemployment. It really does so now through Poor Law, but conditions under which this system has hitherto worked have been so harsh and humiliating that working class pride revolts against accepting so degrading and doubtful a boon. Gradually the obligation of the state to find labour or sustenance will be realised . . . Insurance then will be unnecessary." He was looking forward, clearly, to a comprehensive welfare system based on taxation, including an NHS.

Having laid the foundations, Lloyd George did quite a lot later in the way of building upon them. As Minister of Munitions from 1915 to 1916, he was able to use the near-dictatorial powers that wartime legislation gave him to improve working conditions in British factories. As Prime Minister, he made unemployment benefit universal, and in 1919 established the Department of Health under its own minister. But in the immediate postwar period, political and economic conditions did not favour a smooth continuation of his pioneering work before the war, and after his fall from power in 1922 he never had another chance.

All the same, he had done so much that it seems hard to dispute the claim made on his behalf that he *was* the true founder of the British welfare state. If he had not been the person he was, acting as and when he did, the necessary changes would have taken considerably longer to come about, and countless individuals, as well as Britain itself, would have suffered accordingly.

SEEBOHM ROWNTREE
1871–1954

John Veit Wilson

Since his death in 1954, Benjamin Seebohm Rowntree has been remembered better for ideas about poverty which he did not hold than for the better understanding of it which he pioneered. Some authors who refer to him do so only to criticise his "primary poverty" line, and misquote his statistics: many seem to have overlooked Rowntree's own explanations of his concepts and methods. A reconsideration is overdue. It suggests that Rowntree was an important figure in laying foundations for the welfare state because he was the first to show convincingly that the causes of poverty lie in the structural maldistribution of work, incomes and physical and social environments available to people – and not in their consequent behaviour.

Rowntree was a Liberal who believed that the power of the state should be used to lay down minimum standards for living and to protect citizens from falling beneath them, free of the chance evils of the market. But his contribution to politics was not tactical. In the view of his biographer, Asa Briggs, by giving an empirically-founded explanation of poverty, Rowntree permitted a sensible discussion of the causes and consequences, and made it possible to formulate realistic policies. The breakthrough in understanding which Rowntree's work created was this: politicians could no longer evade responsibility for state action against what was seen, by the end of the 19th century, as a major social problem – a threat to the nation's economic efficiency and political stability.

Rowntree was born in 1871. His father, Joseph Rowntree, was a rich Quaker philanthropist who had successfully built up the cocoa business in York, and his mother was a member of the Danish Seebohm family. He attended the Quaker public school in York, and then studied chemistry at Owens College (later to become the university) in Manchester. At the age of 18, he started in the Cocoa Works at York. He remained involved with the works for the rest of his life, at first as a chemist, setting up a laboratory for analyses and research. But later he developed an interest in improving working conditions and management relations with the workers, which he wrote about and which led the administrative theorist, Lyndall Urwick, to call him "the British management movement's greatest pioneer," in recognition of the international reputation he won.

In his private life, Rowntree was a workaholic with a Quaker social conscience. Quakerism blurs the distinction between the religious and the secular. It is more concerned with discovering truth than affirming dogma. The belief that there is "that of God" in everyone leads to the practice of non-violence, the humane treatment of deviants, and a dislike of exploitative relationships. Social problems are a challenge to action: the poor are valuable, too.

The young Rowntree wondered if the methods of natural science could be used to shed light on the hotly disputed question of the causes of the social distress of poverty. It was not his only interest: as a young man he was involved in adult education, and throughout his life kept up a wide range of socially responsible activities in pursuit of his youthful plans both to study social problems and to be active in public life to help solve them. He thus became much in demand in the first four decades of the century as an expert adviser to the Liberal Party and to governments on health, housing, agricultural economics and on unemployment. But in this essay I shall concentrate on the two strands in his work which are of principal importance to the foundations of the welfare state: his exposure of the impersonal causes of poverty, and his measures of minimum income. Both issues remain contentious to the present day. It is important that Rowntree's original work is understood as he intended.

What, then, revolutionised Edwardian thought about poverty? Like his contemporaries, Rowntree accepted the conventional concept of poverty as a visible life-style – what today we might more broadly describe as deprivation. Rowntree's survey criterion of a poor family was one showing "obvious want and squalor," or one where "the pinched faces of the ragged children told their own tale of poverty and privation." The question was not what poverty *was*, but what were the *causes* of people living in a state of poverty.

Most middle class people – the class which Rowntree was addressing – believed that the poor had enough money not to live in obvious want, but instead *chose* to spend their money on social activities such as drinking and gambling. Poverty thus meant a neglect of diet and health, personal appearance and housing. The resulting poor physique and ill-health among the working class were seen as inimical to the production of strong and well-trained workers and soldiers. For the classes who held power and property, the answer to the question of why the poor were poor was critical to their own interests, quite apart from the altruistic concern which some of them, like Rowntree, had for the poor.

Rowntree's survey of the working class population of York in 1899 had two aims. The first was to find out what proportion of the population was living in poverty, and what the causes were. He wanted to see if Charles Booth's findings in London earlier in the 1890s also applied in a provincial town. The second aim was to study and report on the social conditions of the York working class as a whole, particularly their housing conditions and health standards.

For the first aim, Rowntree and his collaborators had to identify and count the poor. They did this by visiting almost all the working class homes in York (that is, excluding the servant-keeping classes), and counting those which looked poor. They visited 11,560 families, a total of 46,754 people (about two-thirds of the population of York), and identified 20,302 as visibly poor. This was 27.84 per cent of the whole population of the city, a proportion similar to the 30.7 per cent which Booth had found in London. It must be noted that although Rowntree asked about earnings from respondents or their employers, or estimated them, neither he nor Booth used any measure of income to identify who the poor were, contrary to what many later writers have asserted.

Rowntree wanted to test whether the appearances of poverty were due to people wasting incomes sufficient to prevent them, or whether they were due to other factors like insufficient incomes. So the crucial question was: What was *insufficient* income?

Any answer was inevitably a matter of judgment. But Rowntree was anxious that the level of "sufficiency" chosen should be one with which the Charity Organisation Society, and other influential proponents of the "improvidence" hypothesis, could not argue by claiming that it was too high and left room for mis-spending. To do this he had to accept, for the sake of an irrefutable case, a proposition he did not himself agree with: the level of minimal income chosen would have to ignore the satisfaction of social and psychological needs, and it would be restricted solely to meeting physiological needs. He could not expect agreement on what were the factors necessary to meet social and psychological needs, let alone how much they would cost. But physiological needs, it was believed, could be reduced to the costs of a minimum diet, clothing, heating and housing. The inclusion of these factors could not be disputed.

Rowntree, therefore, applied his scientific knowledge to devising a diet which could just maintain "merely physical efficiency" in a healthy person. He based it on the latest nutritional research from the United

States. But to show that his diet was not over-generous by British standards, he adapted it so that it was more economical and less attractive than the diet currently given to paupers in British workhouses. He then added sums for rent, clothing, heating and other sundries, based on the most economical but "acceptable" budgets he collected from working class homes in York.

Rowntree called this minimum income level the *primary poverty* line; and he called the condition which the two-thirds of the poor with higher incomes were in, *secondary poverty*. The implication seemed to be that "primary poverty" was excusable, and so the idea of "secondary poverty" acquired the associations of improvidence which had previously attached to poverty as a whole. Rowntree later emphasised that his intention in devising the primary poverty line was to *avoid* arguments about improvidence; it was not a level of income, he said, on which anyone could actually live. Some later writers seem to have overlooked his explanations, and wrongly ascribe to him the view that anyone who looked poor but had an income above the primary poverty line was therefore improvident. Although Rowntree criticised wasteful and indulgent expenditures, he did so irrespective of class and it is quite untrue that he equated secondary poverty with mismanagement: people in that condition had too little money for all the conventional expenditures needed in order not to seem poor. If they had spent more on food or appearances, they would have had less for social participation.

In Rowntree's view, one might understand their priorities for expenditure even if one did not share them: people want to satisfy social conventions and psychological needs, and they may reasonably choose to do so before their physiological needs. While Rowntree agreed that some of the appearances of "secondary poverty" were due to people spending their limited incomes on alcohol or gambling, he also asserted that secondary poverty could be caused by spending on essentials that were not included in his subsistence minimum. Even what the middle class called "wasteful" expenditures were often due to the conditions in which the poor lived. Rowntree's sensitive understanding of the meaning of poverty is conveyed in his commentaries, and in his descriptions of the families he visited. This extract gives the flavour:

"The true significance of poverty varies with its cause. Take the father of a young family who, for a number of years, has earned good wages and lived in a comfortable house and who is suddenly thrown into poverty through unemployment. He hopes that he will soon be back at work, and meanwhile he and his wife and children tighten their belts, and their attitude to life is that of a prosperous family suffering from what they consider temporary misfortune.

"But if the new job fails to materialise, and days of unemployment turn into weeks, and weeks into months, and months into years, the tragic meaning of 'poverty due to unemployment' is brought home to the family. The furniture and the clothes become daily more shabby. Vitality ebbs slowly away and with it all that is implied by the word 'morale.' Life below the poverty line means one thing to the man who has just sunk below it, and something vastly different to the man who has been living below it for months and years."

Once he had designed his primary poverty line, Rowntree applied it to his census of the working class in York. He found that 1,465 families, a total of 7,230 people, depended on incomes at or below this level. This was almost one in ten of the whole population of the city. He put the number in secondary poverty at 13,072. He arrived at this figure by simply deducting the number in primary poverty from the 20,302 identified visibly as being poor.

But he stressed that the division between primary and secondary poverty "is largely a matter of opinion, depending upon the standard of wellbeing which is considered necessary." He pointed out that if he had taken a primary poverty line only two shillings (10p) a week higher, almost half of all the poor would have been in a state of primary poverty, instead of one-third.

Rowntree's data was not precise enough for him to analyse the reasons for the poverty of all the twenty thousand poor people, even if he is often misquoted as having done so. What he did was to produce a detailed analysis of the *immediate* reasons for the poverty of the third of the poor who were in "primary poverty." Just over one-half of them were poor because of low wages in regular work. Nearly a quarter were poor because more than four children depended on the regular family income. About 15 per cent were poor because of the death of the chief wage earner. Only one in twenty were poor because of illness or old age and even fewer because of irregularity of work or unemployment. As far as the remaining two-thirds of poor people were concerned – those in "secondary poverty" – Rowntree could only say that an explanation of causes would depend on a judgment about the adequacy of his minimum standard.

The second aim of Rowntree's survey was to examine the social conditions of the York working class as a whole. What was new about his findings on slum housing and ill-health was the connection he made with poverty. Nearly nine tenths of all the city's working class housing was unsatisfactory in condition or size. But as long as the very poorest were paying nearly a third of their inadequate incomes in rent, they could not afford to pay more to improve their conditions.

The theoretical assumptions about physical efficiency embodied in

Rowntree's primary poverty line were shown in their reality in the much higher morbidity and mortality rates in the poorest areas. His surveys of the heights and weights of nearly 2,000 schoolchildren from working class homes at differing income levels showed how stunted the poorest children of the city were, even by comparison with the better-off working class. At 13 years old, the average differences for boys *within* the working class were 3½ inches and 11 lb. A rough measure of physical condition showed that over half of all children from the poorest homes showed signs of underfeeding and neglect, compared with only one in nine from the better-off working class families. A study of the actual diets eaten by a sample of the whole population showed that lower working class diets were seriously deficient, containing on average a quarter less food than the contemporary experts prescribed for physical efficiency

Rowntree's findings, published in 1901 and reprinted several times, showed, in short, that *by the conventional life-style measure of poverty* nearly three in ten of the York population were poor: underfed, ill-clothed and badly housed. Of these poor people, one-third had incomes too low to meet even physiological needs, and three-quarters of this extreme poverty was caused by regular earnings which were too low to support the family dependent on them. While just under a half of the working class experienced this extreme poverty at one time, many more suffered from it at two or three stages of their lives, particularly while growing up – because of what Rowntree called the "five alternating periods of want and comparative plenty," during which the family income per head fluctuated because of changes in the number of dependent children and the earning power of the breadwinner.

Nor was poverty merely an urban problem: it was national. In 1913, Rowntree and May Kendall published an analysis of the budgets of a sample of agricultural labourers. This showed that their work was among the very lowest paid, and that their housing conditions were appalling.

Although Rowntree avoided precise policy prescriptions in his book, preferring to let the bare facts stand apart from conclusions his readers might reject, he wrote that the eventual elimination of squalor and the other sufferings of the poor were matters which would involve the use of state power to redistribute wealth. If the state considered the causes of poverty (low pay, inadequate income maintenance and bad housing) as evils which attacked its national efficiency, then the state itself must attack these causes, since it lay beyond the power of the poor to do so themselves.

Rowntree's evidence fed powerfully into the contemporary arguments about "national efficiency." It contributed to the agitation for change which resulted in the first attempts by government (and, in particular, Lloyd George) to cope with the problems on a national scale: old age pensions, sickness and unemployment insurance, school meals and health care, and Trade Boards (which, like the present-day Wages Councils, were supposed to tackle low pay). The statistician, Arthur Bowley and many more replicated Rowntree's survey in other towns and confirmed his conclusions, while others were stimulated by Rowntree's work to report on the national distribution of employment, incomes and wealth, demonstrating the gross disparities.

During the first world war, Lloyd George commissioned Rowntree to oversee the welfare of the workers in the munitions industry, and to help to plan postwar housing policy. His work helped to provide the evidence for the need to oblige local authorities to provide adequate but cheap housing, subsidised by government so that the poor could afford the rents.

In considering the war workers' conditions, Rowntree also studied the possibilities of a minimum wages policy. His calculations were published as *The Human Needs of Labour* in 1918, and extensively revised in 1937. Both versions were based on surveys of the actual budgets of working class households, augmented by a "minimum but conventional" diet, more generous than in 1899. He also allowed for the cost of a higher standard of housing than most people occupied, and for some social spending. The total represented a recommendation for a minimum wage large enough to cover the needs of a family with three dependent children. The family would live at a higher standard while there were fewer children, and Rowntree called for children's allowances if there were more. Ignoring housing costs, this sum was nearly half as much again in real terms as was the "primary poverty" line for the same household.

Rowntree carried out a second survey of York in 1936. His idea was to study the changes in working class life, and he covered a wide range: only a third of this report was directly concerned with poverty. He showed that male average real wages had risen by a third since 1899. Using his minimum wage levels as a new "relative" poverty line, he found that, although "primary poverty" fell from 9.9 per cent to 3.9 per cent of the York population, "*about* 40 per cent of the working class population of York are living below the minimum standard." This was nearly a quarter of the whole population (and not the 18 per cent often wrongly quoted). The principal causes were inadequate pay (one-third); unemployment (over a quarter); and old age (although probably a third of the old in York were *not* poor). Rowntree spelled out the policy conclusions: full employment; higher benefits and pensions; statutory minimum wages and family allowances.

The findings of the 1936 survey were published in 1941, as William Beveridge was about to prepare his famous report. No one can read the Beveridge report without being struck by Rowntree's influence on its assumptions. He was consulted on the calculation of benefit rates and advised against the use of the "primary poverty" concept which Beveridge had favoured. But the report finally proposed cash levels far below Rowntree's 1936 poverty line: 22 shillings a week (£1.10) for a couple, for example, as against Rowntree's 31 shillings 11 pence (£1.60).

In 1950, when he was almost 80, Rowntree carried out a third survey of York with G.R. Lavers. This also affected ideas of the welfare state. Professor A.B. Atkinson and his colleagues have shown that, for methodological reasons, Rowntree probably under-estimated the scale of poverty in his third survey. Had its persistence been realised then, there might have been neither the confidence in the post-Attlee years that the welfare state had virtually abolished poverty, nor the subsequent cynicism when poverty was "re-discovered" 15 years later (for example, by Peter Townsend and Brian Abel-Smith).

Rowntree has been undervalued because of the false belief that he promoted only minimum subsistence measures of poverty. But that part of his work was done simply to convince a reluctant middle class that the deprivation of millions of people was caused not by individual fecklessness but by too little money even for physical survival. When he defended the scientific integrity of his primary poverty line, it was against critics of its generosity.

He always maintained that his poverty lines were minima, intended to focus attention and action on the most urgent problems. He acknowledged that, as conventions changed, so any idea of the acceptable minimum must rise as well, and must be guaranteed by the state. His work on health and housing was also a foundation for state involvement in their provision, and for the empirical approaches to poverty which study the levels of income which correlate with deprivation.

Rowntree's real concerns, however, were not just with money, but with the fulfilment of the whole person. To tolerate the persistence of the suffering caused by poverty was incompatible with Rowntree's Quakerism. It was state officials, and not Rowntree himself, who turned his eye-opening minimum levels into blind maximum incomes. After 80 years, Rowntree's concerns are still lively in any consideration of the boundaries of the tolerable.

ELEANOR RATHBONE
1872–1946

Jane Lewis

In late 19th century Liverpool the family name of Rathbone was synonymous with good works and charitable endeavour. The Rathbone wealth came from a large importing and shipping business, but, like many deeply religious businessmen of his time, William Rathbone VI gradually became more involved in the world of philanthropy than of commerce.

Born in 1872, his daughter Eleanor began her career with voluntary work among Liverpool's poor, and like many other political and social reformers of the period, she became convinced that the state should bear a larger responsibility for welfare provision, although the part that feminism played in the development of her thinking marked her off from her contemporaries. By her death in 1946 she had witnessed the successful end of her famous campaign for family allowances and the emergence of a society where provision for the poor had become primarily a collective rather than a private responsibility.

She went to Oxford in 1893, where she came into contact with the T.H. Green idealist school of philosophy, which made undergraduates devote considerable attention to social problems. The school exerted a strong sway over people studying at Oxford in the late 19th and early 20th centuries. In keeping with the image of the "new woman" of the 1890s, she was a keen feminist. But unlike the daring heroines of some of the novels of the period, she apparently had an "imperturbable unconcern with sex." Like many feminists of her generation, she viewed sex with a distaste that easily turned into disgust and horror when she discovered what she referred to as the "primitive ideas of marital rights which still prevail among the worst sort of (working class) husbands," or the practice of child marriage in India.

After Oxford, she returned to Liverpool without a degree because the Oxford of 1896 did not grant them to women. (She had to wait until 1938 for an honorary DCL.) She was immediately drawn into the Liverpool Central Relief Society as a visitor, and began to write regular notes to her father on the proper administration of charitable relief.

In the late 1890s, Eleanor Rathbone's ideas mirrored those of the Charity Organisation Society. If the poor were to be encouraged in the habits of thrift, then it was disastrous to give them relief to tide them over such misfortunes as "the wife's annual confinement." Her attitude towards poverty gradually changed, in part as a result of her empirical investigations into social problems; in part because of her constant contact with the poor as a visitor and as manager of the Granby Street council school; and in part because of her growing interest in the fight for women's suffrage and in the problems of working class wives.

Moreover, in the particular issues she took up, her approach was in advance of mainstream opinion. In her inquiry into dock labour, published in 1904, she was thinking ahead of Beveridge, who acknowledged her lead in his 1909 analysis of unemployment. Her most original contribution, and the one for which she is best remembered, was her analysis of the need for family allowances, and the campaign she mounted for them which began in 1917 and ended in 1945.

All her work between the wars serves to reflect the fundamental importance of her feminism. She said that it was her distress over the question of Indian child marriage that led her into parliament as an Independent MP for the Combined English Universities in 1929. Certainly, her promotion of the zionist cause – which, together with her campaigns on behalf of Indian women, refugees and the League of Nations, took up more time than the domestic campaign for family allowances – started because of her interest in giving Jewish women in Palestine the vote. She felt she could not but support the cause of a race which had accorded women "the fruits of western emancipation," against that of the Arabs who maintained "the traditions of female subjection, purdah seclusion, the veil and child marriage."

In her own view, her feminism represented a departure from the older egalitarian feminist tradition. In 1919, she took over from Millicent Garrett Fawcett as President of the National Union of Societies for Equal Citizenship, formerly the major constitutional suffrage society. After the vote was granted in 1918, the organisation sought new goals, and it was Eleanor Rathbone's opinion that "to the new school of feminists the habit of continually measuring women's wants by men's achievements seems out-of-date, ignominious and intolerably boring." Now that women had achieved citizenship, she urged them not to copy men's models but to make their own. In particular, she was anxious that women's contribution as mothers should receive due recognition. Early in her presidency of the NUSEC, she criticised the complacency of certain middle class feminists who had got all they wanted out of the women's movement when it gave them the vote, and the right to stand for parliament and to enter the professions. She urged them to think of the position of women who chose to stay at home.

Above all, she had in mind the plight of the working class mother. She had studied the position of widows in Liverpool in 1913, and her discoveries made a powerful impression on her. When arguing for a higher widow's pension than the one the government proposed to give in 1925, she declared that she was thinking of the "faces which float before my mind of the women whom I used to know 20-30 years ago . . . The lives they led were harder and drearier than anything we comfortable people have ever experienced. Some had their children, others seemed to have nothing, nor hope of anything but to be able to go stitching or scrubbing till they died." Her passionate concern for the conditions of working class mothers was exceptional. Both her public and private life were generally marked by a profound reserve.

Her case for family allowances was fully expressed in *The Disinherited Family*, published in 1924. This remarkable book challenged both male-dominated economic theory and men's privileged position within the family. She charged economists with ignoring the economics of the family: "I do not think it would be an exaggeration to say that, if the population of Great Britain consisted entirely of adult self-propagating bachelors and spinsters, nearly the whole output of writers on economic theory during the past 50 years might remain as it was written." She was the first to explore the implications for women and children of the notions of a male breadwinner and a "family wage" – ie, the idea that what is paid to a man is necessarily enough for the whole family. These concepts have been recently rediscovered by the feminist movement.

Earlier social investigators, such as Seebohm Rowntree, had argued that the low-paid worker with a large family could not possibly build up sufficient savings to see him and his family through sickness, unemployment and old age, and had gone on to call for a living wage based on the needs of the "average" family of five (two adults and three children). Rathbone's first step was to explode the myth of the average family of five. Only 8.8 per cent of families fell into this category in 1924. Thus Rathbone pointed out that if a living wage for all were calculated on this basis it would make provision for non-existent children in the case of 52 per cent of workers, while still not doing enough to help the 9.9 per cent of families with more than three children.

But it was not just the inability of the wage system to provide for all sizes and kinds of families (including those headed by women), over all phases of the family life-cycle, that concerned Eleanor Rathbone. She also objected strongly to economic theorists treating the family not as an aggregate of individual human beings, but as dependants and bread-winners. She believed that the economic dependency of women and children reduced them to the status of male luxuries. Family allowances represented the mother's claim to a dignified and secure economic status.

In her early formulations, she proposed that wages should be based on the needs of a single person, and that cash allowances should be paid to the mother, as well as to each child, in recognition of her work in the home – an early call for wages for housework. Later she dropped the allowance for the mother, and advocated a wage sufficient for two people, largely because she feared that an allowance for the mother might be used to exclude women from the labour market. She never wanted family allowances paid only to women who stayed at home, even though, in common with most feminists of her generation, she believed that motherhood was incompatible with work outside the home.

She also believed that allowances would help the position of single women. Once children were made economically independent of men, the chief impediment to equal pay for women working outside the home would be removed. Men would no longer be able to claim extra pay for the same job on the grounds that they had a family to support.

Her arguments against the family wage were strongly attacked from all sides. Economists and social investigators feared that removing the responsibility for providing from the male breadwinner would have a disastrous effect on male work incentives. Ramsay MacDonald regar-ded the idea of family allowances as "an insane outburst of indi-vidualism," and declared that under socialism the mother and child-ren's rights to maintenance would be honoured by the family, not the state.

Trade unionists feared, rightly, the impact that allowances would have on wage levels. Eleanor Rathbone failed to stress the importance of keeping the issue of allowances separate from wage negotiating, and regarded male trade unionist opposition as proof of the male desire to dominate, which she referred to as the "Turk complex":

"A man likes to feel that he has 'dependants.' He looks in the glass and sees himself as perhaps others see him – physically negligible, mentally ill-equipped, poor, unimportant, unsuccessful. He looks in the mirror he keeps in his mind, and sees his wife clinging to his arm and the children clustered round her skirts; all looking up to him, as that giver of all good gifts, the wage-earner. The picture is very alluring."

Eleanor Rathbone advocated a gradualist approach to social change and had no patience with those who thought otherwise. (Her work on behalf of Indian women was severely hampered by her failure to understand the strength of Indian nationalism.) She ran her campaign for family allowances in the classic manner of the suffragist societies, working through the small Family Endowment Society she founded in 1917. She concentrated on aiming for the maximum achievable, on being early in the field, and on lobbying energetically and with "the perseverence of Sisyphus, Bruce's spider, the Ancient Mariner and the Importunate Widow, all rolled into one." The society tried to convert people from all political persuasions. It used every opportunity to promote consideration of family needs by ministers and public servants. It proposed, for example, a scheme of rent rebates for inclusion in the 1930s housing legislation.

During the 1930s, the feminist case for allowances tended to become submerged beneath "family poverty" and demographic arguments as the Family Endowment Society became an umbrella organisation for those "committed to the principle of direct provision for the family," no matter what their motive. In common with many organisations and individuals, Eleanor Rathbone made good use of new research into nutritional needs to argue for higher unemployment benefits and the distribution of foods, especially milk, to mothers and children. In 1934, she founded a second organisation, the Children's Minimum Council, to work expressly for scales of unemployment benefit and assistance which would enable families to purchase the diet recommended by the BMA. The council and the Family Endowment Society were the only political pressure groups for the family before the Child Poverty Action Group.

Demographic arguments in favour of allowances tended to appeal chiefly to conservatives. Rathbone agreed with the members of the Eugenics Education Society that they were right to abhor any policy that might result in an increase in population "of the wrong kind." But she assured them that by improving the status of the mother, family allowances would help stem "the devastating torrent of children" from the working class, while perhaps encouraging the more prudent middle classes to have more children. After all, Beveridge, an early convert to family allowances, introduced an allowance scheme at the London School of Economics in an effort to raise the birth rate among academic staff. Rathbone herself had no hesitation in welcoming the possibility of population control via the manipulation of family allowances, which she referred to as the state putting its hand on "the tiller of maternity."

Her underlying conservatism, and readiness to contemplate a large measure of state paternalism, was also apparent in the way in which her early writing envisaged allowances being made conditional on good mothercraft. Nor did she wish allowances to go to unmarried mothers.

Like many present-day advocates of policies to support the family, she had a clear idea of the kind of family she wished to be supported.

She was prepared to use any argument to further the cause of family allowances, and was ready to address both the political right and left, miners and eugenicists. She worked with the extremely conservative Duchess of Atholl in her campaigns on behalf of Indian women and against female circumcision in Africa, and with socialists such as Mary Stocks and H.N. Brailsford in the movement for family allowances. But it would be wrong to regard her as a political opportunist, or even as a simple pragmatist.

Most of her contemporaries would have agreed with Edith Summerskill's assessment of her as a fine, moral and principled individual. Moreover, her initial analysis of family dependency related the problems it raised to the social and economic system in a manner that has been rare amongst those seeking to reduce or ameliorate poverty. But having decided that family allowances offered a solution, the Rathbone belief in "whatever can be done ought to be done" took over, and the principle of family allowances was pursued to the exclusion of all other considerations.

When family allowances were granted in 1945, the legislation owed little to the arguments of Rathbone and the Family Endowment Society although their importance in keeping the idea at the forefront of debate should not be under-estimated. Interwar governments were determined not to recognise the validity of the most widely debated argument in favour of allowances – that of "family poverty." All government departments agreed that it was politically impossible to admit that families drawing relief were unable to afford a medically approved minimum diet. Moreover, both the Family Endowment Society and the Children's Minimum Council were primarily women's pressure groups. Government departments felt it safe to ignore them.

When Lord Balniel attended the opening meeting of the Children's Minimum Council in 1934 on behalf of the Ministry of Health, he dismissed it as "a number of disappointed spinsters, representing 'many millions' of mothers, [who] advocated all the old demands for free milk, etcetera, for nursing mothers, etcetera, etcetera."

The government began to take family allowances seriously at the beginning of the second world war as a means of holding down wages, and because it realised that it had to deal with the question of men with big families who were better off when they were out of work. The problem of overlap between wages and unemployment assistance and benefits emerged during the late 1930s, whereupon it became possible to turn previous arguments on their head, and claim family allowances as the best way of preserving work incentives.

Only one small part of the original feminist proposal for allowances was achieved in 1945. The bill proposed to give the allowance to the father rather than the mother, but Rathbone warned that "sex grievance" would play a major part in the next election if this were done. On a free vote, the decision was taken to pay allowances to the mother.

Ministers and civil servants never intended family allowances to cover the full costs of maintaining a child. They gradually fell behind the rate of inflation. After 1945 low unemployment and rising real wages permitted governments to ignore the economics of the family. The turning point came in the 1960s when researchers like Peter Townsend and Brian Abel-Smith gave poverty a "relative" definition. Attention focused on family allowances again.

But the problems identified by Eleanor Rathbone remain. It is still true that a half of all male wage earners have no dependants, while the vast increase in the number of families headed by women has made the demand for a fair share for women and children more rather than less urgent. As Hilary Land has commented, she would be dismayed to find that today the tax subsidy to marriage, which mainly benefits married men, is roughly equivalent to the cost of the state's financial support to parents in general, and certainly more than that paid directly to mothers.

Towards the end of the 1970s, feminists examining the relationship between women's position in the labour force and in the family, began to re-explore the concept of the family wage. Like Eleanor Rathbone, they pointed out that the assumption of a male breadwinner makes it possible for male workers to claim more pay, and also for the social security system to ignore the crucial economic contribution married women workers make to the family economy. Recent feminist analysis has gone one stage further than Rathbone in demanding not only an equal economic relationship between men and women, but also an equal division of labour within the family in the work of caring for children, the sick, the old and otherwise dependent relatives and in household chores.

Rathbone's belief in gradualism led her to promote family allowances as an essentially ameliorative reform. But if her analysis of the economics of the family is pushed as feminists are currently doing, then it raises fundamental questions regarding the way in which work is defined – within the family as well as at the workplace – and the function and source of the wage.

WILLIAM BEVERIDGE
1879–1963

Tony Lynes

In the 18 chapters of her magnificent biography of William Beveridge, Jose Harris devotes one chapter to the making of the Beveridge report and one to its aftermath. In relation to the achievements of a long and varied career, that is a fair allocation of space. But for most people the name of Beveridge is indissolubly linked to the report on *Social Insurance and Allied Services* which, published in the middle of a world war, provided a blueprint for social policy in the years of peace. It is a remarkable fact that, 40 years later, discussion of the strengths and weaknesses of the British social security system is still conducted largely in terms of the principles enunciated by Beveridge. Indeed, it is only in recent years that criticism has turned from the failure of successive governments to implement those principles to the questioning of the principles themselves.

Beveridge's claim to be seen as one of the founding fathers of the British welfare state rests, however, on much more than the *Social Insurance* report. It is arguable that his most original and fundamental contribution to social policy was made in the early years of the century when his energies were largely devoted to the causes and cures of unemployment. And it was to this subject that he returned during the second world war when, in *Full Employment in a Free Society*, he followed up *Social Insurance* with a detailed exposition of the policies required not to cure but to prevent unemployment in postwar Britain. It was a radical document, strongly influenced by Keynesian ideas, and the coalition government was sufficiently alarmed to rush out its own white paper on full employment in an attempt to distract attention from Beveridge's ideas.

On leaving Oxford in 1903, Beveridge became sub-warden of the East End settlement, Toynbee Hall, at a time when unemployment was a major problem. Disillusioned by philanthropic attempts to help the unemployed, he soon became convinced of the need for government action. Within a few years he was the acknowledged expert on the subject, and his views were expounded in his first book, *Unemployment: a Problem of Industry* (1909). "Everyone," he wrote, "has seen in a window at times the notice, 'Boy Wanted.' No one, it is safe to say, has ever seen in a window the notice 'Boots Wanted'." Labour, unlike boots, was sold by the inefficient method of hawking it from door to door. Unemployment and under-employment were symptoms of the inefficiency of the labour market. The cure he proposed was a system of labour exchanges "to which employers shall send or go when they want workpeople, to which workpeople shall go when they want employment."

In his enthusiasm for labour exchanges, Beveridge certainly exaggerated their efficacy as a means of preventing unemployment. On the other hand, he could not foresee the long-term structural unemployment that was to characterise the interwar period. Labour, like boots, can only be sold if there is someone willing to buy it. In a situation of mass unemployment, the exchanges inevitably degenerated into mere dole offices.

Unemployment insurance was an integral part of Beveridge's proposals. "The Labour Exchange is required to reduce to a minimum the intervals between successive jobs. Insurance is required to tide over the intervals that will still remain." Trade union benefit schemes already existed but the lack of any effective test of willingness to work prevented the unions from paying adequate benefits. Labour exchanges would solve this problem, whether benefits were in future provided by the unions or by the state.

In choosing insurance as the instrument by which financial support for the unemployed was to be provided, Beveridge was no doubt influenced by the trade union schemes. But there was more to it than that. His interest in social insurance went back to 1907 when Asquith, as Chancellor of the Exchequer, promised to introduce old age pensions. Only a year before, Beveridge had commented that compulsory insurance on the German model entailed "an amount of regulation and identification of individuals entirely foreign to British habits." But a visit to Germany converted him into a lifelong advocate of social insurance. By 1942 he was able to write that "benefit in return for contributions, rather than free allowances from the State, is what the people of Britain desire."

Beveridge had left Toynbee Hall in 1905 to write on social questions for the *Morning Post*, a job which enabled him to pursue his studies of the facts and causes of unemployment while giving him a highly respectable platform from which to propound his solutions. But his big opportunity came in July 1908 when Winston Churchill, newly appointed President of the Board of Trade, invited him to become a full-time official and help to create a system of labour exchanges. A year later the Labour Exchanges Act was passed, and in February 1910 the exchanges opened their doors. Beveridge, meanwhile, was working with the Board of Trade's permanent secretary, Sir Hubert Llewellyn Smith, on the details of the unemployment insurance scheme that was to become part II of the National Insurance Bill, 1911.

Although he played an important role in planning the insurance scheme, labour exchanges were to a much greater extent the result of his personal efforts. To have become, by the age of 30, the main architect of a major piece of social legislation and of the administrative machinery resulting from it was a remarkable achievement, but one which did little to prepare him for the frustrations that are the more usual lot of a social reformer in the British civil service. Although he remained a civil servant until 1919 and had by then reached the rank of permanent secretary, his appointment as director of the London School of Economics – a post he held from 1919 until 1937 – came as a "glorious relief."

Beveridge was not directly involved in social insurance in the 1920s, but in 1924 he read Eleanor Rathbone's book, *The Disinherited Family*, and was instantly converted to the cause of family allowances. He promptly introduced them for the staff of the LSE. The following year, as a member of the Samuel Commission on the coal industry, he urged the adoption of family allowances as an immediate means of improving the lot of the miners without adding to the wage bill.

Beveridge's support for family allowances was consistent with his whole approach to social policy. As early as 1905 he had rejected the view that poverty was an unalterable economic fact. The problem was to find ways of redistributing resources in favour of the poor. Family allowances were a singularly attractive, because wholly rational, way of doing this. They were consistent, also, with his view that the right way to abolish poverty was to give people an adequate income and leave them to spend it. After a Toynbee Hall conference on free school meals in 1904, he wrote,"Granted that many parents have now the responsibility of feeding their children without the power of doing so (through low wages) the remedy is not to remove the responsibility but to give the power." And in the 1942 Beveridge report he wrote, "Management of one's income is an essential element of a citizen's freedom."

His belief in family allowances as a necessary element in a rational distribution of incomes was strongly reinforced by his experience from 1934 on as chairman of the Unemployment Insurance Statutory Committee. This body was set up as part of the process of restoring the financial basis of unemployment insurance after the 1931 collapse. Its job was to keep a watch on the scheme's solvency and advise on changes in contributions and benefits. In 1935, the committee recommended an increase in the allowance for the child of an unemployed man from 2 to 3 shillings a week. It pointed out that this would bring the total benefit for a man with a wife and five children up to 41 shillings a week, while a man with eight or ten children would get 50 or 56 shillings a week, at a time when many unskilled workers earned about 40 shillings. They therefore proposed a benefit ceiling of 41 shillings, which would mean that no further additions would be payable after the fifth child.

The government decided to implement the increase in the children's allowance but not the benefit ceiling. The committee did not pursue the question of a benefit ceiling, but remarked in its next report: "The growing direct provision for families, under unemployment insurance and assistance, is beginning to raise acutely the general problem of dependency, under a wage system which makes no similar provision." Thus Beveridge became convinced of the need for family allowances as a pre-condition of adequate social insurance benefits, and their introduction was to be one of the three "assumptions" on which the proposals of the Beveridge report rested. The other two were full employment and a national health service.

By 1941, when Beveridge was asked to chair an inquiry into the various existing schemes of social insurance, he was again, as he had been 30 years earlier, an acknowledged expert on unemployment insurance. His knowledge of health insurance, pensions and workmen's compensation was less detailed, but the new committee of which he was to be chairman consisted entirely of officials from the government departments concerned, and was therefore of a highly expert character. And as well as his own knowledge and experience, Beveridge brought to the job a growing belief in the need for, and the possibility of, a degree of social and economic planning unknown in prewar (or, in fact, postwar) Britain.

The background to his new assignment was a curious one. He had been brought into the Ministry of Labour by Ernest Bevin in 1940, but the arrangement was not a happy one. Jose Harris records that Bevin at first opposed the social insurance inquiry but "changed his mind when he saw that it was a chance of ridding himself of Beveridge." As for Beveridge, though at first bitterly disappointed at being "kicked upstairs" in this way, he gradually came to realise that he had been presented with a golden opportunity to produce a comprehensive plan for social reform. He seized it with both hands. It soon became apparent that the kind of report Beveridge intended to produce could not be signed by a committee of officials. The other members of the committee therefore became "advisers and assessors," and the report was signed by Beveridge alone. Its impact, both at the time of publication and subsequently, was so great that even now, like the Bible, it is difficult to read and assess it dispassionately.

Most of the report consists of very detailed proposals about the benefits to be provided, the means of financing them, the machinery of administration, and so on. But they are presented in a manner which is far removed from the sober style of most official reports. To quote just the last sentence of Beveridge's peroration, in which he urges that action to implement his plan should not be deferred until after the war:

"The Plan for Social Security in this Report is submitted by one who believes that in this supreme crisis the British people will not be found wanting, of courage and faith and national unity, of material and spiritual power to play their part in achieving both social security and the victory of justice among nations upon which security depends."

Behind the rhetoric, what did the report amount to? A mere tidying-up operation, as some have suggested, or something more?

To talk of "mere" tidying-up in this context is misleading. Historical accident had given no less than seven government departments an interest in one or more cash benefits. And it was not just the administrative machinery that needed tidying. The benefits themselves varied widely, and the variations bore little relation to the needs of the recipients. For example, a married man with two children was entitled to more than twice as much in unemployment as in sickness. In the health insurance scheme, administration of benefits by "approved societies" which could spend their surpluses on additional benefits created further inequalities. Bringing some order into this chaos was a long overdue task.

There were also glaring gaps in the scope of existing schemes. Higher paid non-manual workers were not insured; nor were the self-employed. Some important areas were covered only by commercial insurance: funeral benefits and workmen's compensation for industrial accidents fell in this category and both were in urgent need of reform.

Beveridge was too much of a realist to imagine that the existing schemes could simply be swept away. But he was enough of a visionary to see that, if the anomalies were to be removed, there must be a grand new scheme into which the best of what already existed could be fitted. And if his proposals were to stand any chance of being carried against the powerful vested interests involved, and of gaining the necessary resources from a reluctant Treasury, they must be presented in a way which would mobilise public opinion behind a few simple and idealistic principles.

The report brilliantly succeeded in doing that. It is here that its true greatness lies. But it would be wrong to under-estimate it as a straightforward and business-like investigation of an extremely complex area of social policy. Behind the rhetoric is to be found most of the National Insurance Act of 1946 and much of the social security scheme which, for better or for worse, we still have.

The report has been criticised as backward-looking. In a sense it was. It set out to correct the errors of the past, and to remedy the inadequacies of existing provision, rather than to create something totally new. Thus the system of flat-rate benefits was to be retained. But the levels of benefit were to be based on the subsistence needs of the family. Whether Beveridge's estimates of subsistence needs were adequate is another question. But they were certainly believed to be so at the time.

To go beyond subsistence would have meant either recommending a higher level of flat-rate benefits, or abandoning the flat-rate approach in favour of benefits related to individual earnings. Flat-rate benefits above subsistence were not, in the circumstances, a realistic option. Even at the levels proposed, Beveridge had to concede a 20 year phasing-in of full subsistence pensions as the price of grudging acceptance of his plan by the Treasury. And although that concession was rejected by the Attlee government, the postwar benefit rates still fell short of the subsistence target represented by the national assistance scale.

As for earnings-related benefits, Beveridge realised that his proposals were out of harmony with the development of social security elsewhere. He also realised that flat-rate benefits by themselves were not enough. The system of flat-rate benefits, he explained, "follows from the recognition of the place and importance of voluntary insurance in social security and distinguishes the scheme proposed for Britain from the security schemes of Germany, the Soviet Union, the United States and most other countries with the exception of New Zealand." Yet he was well aware of the limitations of voluntary (mainly commercial) insurance, and it is a major weakness of the report that he seems to have given no thought to the reforms that would be needed in order to justify reliance on voluntary insurance as a supplement to subsistence benefits. He dismissed private superannuation schemes in one short paragraph, concluding that "no special action by the State is called for." Yet he had himself suffered from the non-transferability of civil service pensions on moving to the LSE in 1919.

Would it have been better, therefore, to break away from the flat-rate basis of the 1911 act, and recommend a system of earnings-related social security? Perhaps it would, though the difficulty of selling such a novel and apparently inegalitarian concept would have been formidable. But what would then have become of the subsistence aim? Would pensions have been raised from 10 shillings (50p) to 26 shillings

(£1.30p) a week in 1946, as they were, if the government had at the same time been preparing for the introduction of an earnings-related scheme which, as is the way with such schemes, would have given nothing to the existing generation of pensioners? And how attractive would earnings-related unemployment benefit have seemed when the earnings of most of the prospective unemployed consisted of army pay?

If Beveridge was right to stick to flat-rate subsistence benefits, was he also right to stick to social insurance, with rights based on contributions paid, as the framework of his plan? Again, the question must be put in context. He believed that the quasi-contractual basis of social insurance offered greater security than a system financed by taxes. Tax-financing, on the other hand, was more likely to bring an extension of means testing of which he was a life-long opponent.

The fact that these beliefs may no longer hold good 40 years later does not mean that they were wrong in 1942. Where Beveridge was wrong was in allowing the insurance principle to become not just a protection but a straitjacket. One of the main potential advantages of flat-rate benefits is that the link between the individual's contribution record and his benefit rights can be extremely tenuous or even, where the circumstances demand it, non-existent. For example, Beveridge's insistence that sickness benefit should be earned by a minimum number of contributions actually paid meant that permanently disabled people who had never worked could not, and still cannot, claim insurance benefits.

Less defensible than the contributory principle itself was the decision that flat-rate benefits must be financed by flat-rate contributions. Some of those giving evidence to the Beveridge committee favoured graduated contributions for flat-rate benefits. But Beveridge had no time for such ideas: "The tradition of the fixed price is very strong in this country. You do not like having to pay more than your neighbours." Yet in the report itself he wrote, "The Plan for Social Security is first and foremost a method of redistributing income." Moreover, his proposals for financing the plan included a large and growing contribution paid by the Exchequer out of general taxation. The idea that everybody was to pay the same for equal benefits was a pure fiction, which would have been better abandoned from the outset.

Many other criticisms have been levelled at Beveridge's proposals in the past 40 years. His views about the status of married women were archaic. He failed to recognise the needs of one-parent families. His plan did not provide for the costs of disablement. But if Beveridge made mistakes, we have had 40 years to put them right. Perhaps it is time we stopped blaming Beveridge for our own failures, and gave him the recognition he deserves for transforming the rickety structure of prewar social security into a building whose foundations have proved remarkably solid.

R.H. TAWNEY
1880–1962

J.M. Winter

The name of R.H. Tawney was honoured in 1982 in a way which would have amused no one more than Tawney himself. If spectres have access to the *Guardian* or *The Times*, a billowing cloud of pipe tobacco may have appeared in the sky around the time that eminent members of the Social Democratic Party formed a Tawney Society and claimed him as their spiritual progenitor.

The subsequent quarrel between Labour Party loyalists and Social Democrats about where Tawney's spiritual bones should lie bears a resemblance to the medieval practice of disinterring the remains of saints. But underlying the claims and counter-claims of intellectual kinship or descent, there is a more serious question at hand. What was the essence of Tawney's egalitarian socialism, and where does it lead politically?

The first and most striking characteristic of Tawney's socialism was his identification of the class struggle as the struggle against privilege. This was a notion widely shared by many people born in the late Victorian period who migrated to the cause of Fabian socialism or the "New Liberalism." The world which they inherited, and which they worked to change, was steeped in privilege. Tawney and most of his generation were deeply aware of that simple fact. They knew that the accident of birth had set them far apart from the mass of the population.

Precisely how far apart was vividly illustrated in the writings of Charles Booth, Seebohm Rowntree, and Mrs Pember Reeves, author of *Round about a Pound a Week*, among others. Such publications made it clear to anyone with eyes to see what privilege meant, by exposing the stark contrasts in life chances between men and women of different social strata. The literature of social observation, and the anxious appraisals of defenders of the future of the empire, documented the conditions which accounted for the fact that over one in five children born in most major industrial centres in Britain in 1900 failed to survive the first year of life. The human meaning of privilege was reflected in the differential toll of malnutrition and disease. In 1911, the infant mortality rate of children of unskilled workers was double that of children of professional men.

Such a waste of life occurred at a time when the nation's economy was still in a relatively strong, though not unchallenged, position. A stable currency and a booming export trade made it possible for pre-1914 Britain to be at once the financial capital of the world and the home of some of the worst slums in Europe. Many of Tawney's contemporaries were troubled by this paradox. They asked why it was necessary for working class children to be poorly fed, poorly housed, inadequately educated in elementary schools designed for the restricted "needs" of the labouring class, thrown on the labour market early in adolescence, frequently in dead-end jobs, then to reach a maturity in which they too could have a family destined to repeat the cycle of deprivation.

How different it was for men of Tawney's class, whose control over the conditions of their lives seemed to be effortless and complete. Born in India in 1880, the son of a distinguished Sanskrit scholar and principal of Presidency College in Calcutta, raised in comfort in Surrey, educated at Rugby and Balliol, Tawney had all that the pedigree of privilege could provide. Why did he not accept his good fortune as an act of providence and settle down to a sedate and complacent sinecure appropriate to this station in life?

There can never be a complete answer to this question, whether it be applied to Tawney or to others who have troubled the conventional order in the past. But in Tawney's case (as elsewhere), it may be that the key sources of rebellion lay in the subversive character of certain religious beliefs.

Tawney's Anglican convictions were the foundation of much of his egalitarian philosophy. In this he joined a tradition which combined elements of Calvinist theology and Puritan zeal, tempered in the crucible of the English Civil War. After a long hibernation, this cast of mind re-emerged in mid-Victorian England in the writings of John Ruskin and Matthew Arnold and in the Christian Socialist movement. Tawney's major essays in political philosophy, *The Acquisitive Society* (1921) and *Equality* (1931), constitute a distinctive contribution to the cause of Christian idealism.

To assert, as Tawney did in 1912, that "In order to believe in equality, it is necessary to believe in God" was to reveal the characteristic flavour of his political position. To Tawney, the privileges of his class were indefensible in that they arose out of arbitrary distinctions between men on the basis of inherited or acquired wealth. For a Christian, Tawney wrote, such divisions manifested a denial of the truth that all men are equally children of sin and equally insignificant in the eyes of the Lord.

Without a belief in God, it might be possible to accept inequality as either in the nature of things or necessary to human progress. But once the elements of faith intruded, Tawney argued, the capitalist order of inequality was exposed as an irreligious system of individual and collective behaviour, out of which no personal or collective morality acceptable to a Christian could arise. What Matthew Arnold called the "religion of inequality" – "that temper which regarded violent contrasts between the circumstances and opportunities of different classes with respectful enthusiasm, as a phenomenon, not merely inevitable, but admirable and exhilarating" – was really the obverse of a Christian way of looking at the world.

Anglicanism is, of course, a house of many mansions, in which there is room for the ideas of Enoch Powell alongside those of Tawney. The view that capitalism is un-Christian because it stultifies the common fellowship of men of different means and occupations has never been more than a minority view. But over the past century such ideas have been held with conviction by a number of influential Anglicans. Alongside the Labour MP, George Lansbury, and William Temple, Archbishop of Canterbury during the second world war and a life-long friend, Tawney spoke out against capitalism as a way of life which violated the moral precepts of his faith.

Tawney's message was particularly powerful because, in his work as a teacher and planner of educational reform, as a historian, and as an active member of the Labour Party, his voice had a resonance which appealed to many who did not share his religious outlook. This was in part because he wrote with the moral outrage of Marx, but also with the grace and eloquence of Milton. His strength lay, too, in the fact that his was a distinctively English voice. His call for an alternative to the cash nexus struck a chord among many people not of a religious temperament who sought indigenous answers to the problems of a society crippled by the injuries of class.

Tawney was one of the fortunate few who find in their profession a way to express their deepest philosophical concerns. The most important formative experience of his early life was as a teacher of working men. A few years after leaving Oxford, and after brief periods at Toynbee Hall and in Glasgow as a junior lecturer in economics, he found his calling as one of the founders of the Workers' Educational Association.

This organisation grew out of an attempt to prise open the gates of the ancient universities to give to working people the educational opportunities restricted to the privileged few. This objective has never been realised, but as first tutor and perennial inspiration of the WEA, Tawney helped to foster a movement in workers' education in which his egalitarian Anglicanism found its most complete expression. In these evening classes, attended by workers in Rochdale and Longton, he found a fellowship in learning, a society of equals untainted by what he later called "the vulgar irrelevancies of class and income."

In the years before 1914, he also developed an interest in the link between the exploitation of adolescent labour and the inadequacies of the state educational system. Here was the source of his advocacy of secondary education for all, the case for which he propounded in many publications and on many forums. He was the author of most Labour Party statements on education between the wars, a frequent contributor and leader writer for the *Manchester Guardian* on educational questions, and one of those responsible for the Hadow report of 1926 on the education of the adolescent, the principles of which were largely embodied in the 1944 Education Act.

In the same period, he advanced what is still today the radical proposition that the public schools should be incorporated in the state educational system. Here, as in all of his work in education, he acted out of convictions clearly stated in the commonplace book he kept before the first world war. We must begin, Tawney noted in 1912, "to think of knowledge, like religion, as transcending all differences of class and wealth," and to recall "that in the eye of learning, as in the eye of God, all men are equal, because all are infinitely small. To sell education for money is the next thing to selling the gifts of God for money."

The unity of Tawney's work can also be seen in his historical scholarship. Largely through his teaching for the WEA and after 1921 at the London School of Economics, his life-long academic home, he developed a concept of economic history of significant influence today. In his view, the subject entailed the retrieval of the resistance of groups and individuals in the past to the imposition on them of capitalist modes of thought and behaviour.

In his first book, *The Agrarian Problem in the 16th Century* (1912), written to provide his WEA classes with a suitable textbook, he examined patterns of agrarian development, protest and litigation which surrounded the enclosure of land in Tudor England. After an interruption for service in the British army during the 1914–18 war, during which he was severely wounded on the first day of the Battle of the Somme, he returned to historical study, and developed the arguments which were to appear in what is perhaps his best-known book, *Religion and the Rise of Capitalism* (1926). This famous work showed how alien to the teachings of the Reformation was the assumption that religious thought had no bearing on economic behaviour. Tawney captured in unforgettable prose the clash within religious opinion that preceded the abnegation of the social responsibility of the churches, and suggested that "religious indifferentism" was but a phase in the history of Christian thought.

No one who read Tawney could miss the presentmindedness of his history. Indeed it was that very quality which has made his work so attractive to generations of students. He taught them that the study of economic history could raise fundamental questions concerning human behaviour and moral values. Even though many of his conclusions have been subjected to searching criticism, and some have been rejected by later scholars, the period on which he produced his major work is still seen as "Tawney's century," a tribute of which any historian would be proud.

On party political questions, Tawney's commitments were equally clear. There can be no doubt as to the loyalty he felt over 50 years of service to the Labour Party as the political wing of the working class movement. In his early years he did not believe that the Labour Party could accomplish much without a prior shift in popular attitudes to poverty and privilege.

This made him sceptical, too, of the Fabian strategy of permeation and administrative reform, which seemed to him to be concerned more with the mechanics of government than with encouraging the active participation of the governed in the day-to-day business of ordering their lives. Consequently he was drawn to the Utopian ideas of a small group of advocates of workers' control of industry, the guild socialists. These men believed that trade unions could evolve into the agencies of workers' control of production, leaving to the state the work of organising services related to the interests of all citizens as consumers.

The interwar depression swept away the meagre attempts to try to put these ideas into practice. By then, socialists like Tawney were left with a restricted choice in politics. On the one hand was the Communist Party – a tiny group of militants fascinated by the bolshevik revolution and hopelessly isolated from the mainstream of the labour movement. On the other hand was the Labour Party. Tawney unhesitatingly chose the latter, because he believed that English socialism had to speak in the language of English political culture, which was remorselessly and immovably democratic.

Despite the fact that the Labour Party had adopted in its 1918 constitution a commitment to work for the common ownership of the means of production, Tawney had few illusions about the short-term chances of converting this statement of intent into a realistic policy. In a celebrated passage he likened the socialism of the mass membership of the Labour Party to the Christianity of the Chinese soldiers whose general decided to baptise them all with a hose.

It was all the more important, then, for men like Tawney to stay in the Labour Party and to lead by example. Socialism, he believed, could not be realised unless it embodied both "a personal attitude and a collective effort." The recognition of how much work had to be done before the Labour Party could become a socialist party was lacking in the years before the debacle of 1931, when a Labour Prime Minister deserted his party at a time of economic crisis. But even after Labour had begun to rebuild, Tawney argued that it would accomplish little unless its strength consisted of "a body of men and women who, whether trade unionists or intellectuals, put socialism first, and whose creed carries conviction, because they live in accordance with it."

This was no argument for sectarianism, either outside or inside the Labour Party. Indeed, Tawney directed some of his most withering prose against those who lost faith in the Labour Party. To ditch the Labour Party, in the hope of finding a better home for the purist's vision of socialist politics, was to live in a fool's paradise, especially at a time of industrial depression. Writing in 1938, when unemployment in Britain was still above 10 per cent of the labour force, Tawney argued that "socialism is no longer bad politics in England, unless socialists choose to make it so, which some of them do with surprising ingenuity."

Here he was referring to the sectarians within the Labour Party, the Militant Tendency of an earlier day. To the extent that they spoke in a language remote from the democratic assumptions of ordinary people, they were bound to cause more harm than good. But, Tawney went on, "an attitude of heavy-footed heresy-hunting would be the worst way of dealing with them." Democratic socialism had to remain a dialogue if it was to retain its character as a living doctrine.

Of even greater importance for the future of democratic socialism was its need to retain its strong links with the trade union movement. Tawney's work in adult education had brought him into contact with miners and their unions. At the end of the first world war he served on the Sankey Commission on the coal industry, which recommended the end of private ownership.

His case for nationalisation was based on three premises. First, profits derived from the exploitation of the nation's natural resources should be shared by the nation as a whole. Second, the organisation of the industry in private hands was chaotic and hopelessly inefficient. Third, and perhaps of greatest importance, nationalisation was the best hope of realising the aspirations of working men to have a fair share in decisions which affected their working lives.

What the function of trade unionism would be after nationalisation is a question Tawney left largely unanswered. But there is little doubt that he recognised that there was as great a need to guard against the arrogance of managers paid by the state as there was to oppose the dictatorship of private enterprise.

When the Attlee government after 1945 put into effect a sweeping programme of nationalisation and extension of the social services, Tawney had already reached his declining years. But when, in the early 1950s, he surveyed the progress of the political work with which he had been identified for the best part of half a century, he had reason to feel some measure of satisfaction. Tax reform, the establishment of a national health service, and the extension of public educational provision, had mitigated or eliminated many of the vestiges of privilege, the existence of which in the Edwardian period had fired his political will and vision. But Tawney never believed that it was possible to abolish the "religion of inequality" by statute. The war against privilege was bound to continue, in other forms and with other objectives.

Now, 20 years after his death, it is idle to speculate on precisely what Tawney would advocate in British politics today. But of this we can be sure. He believed that the struggle against privilege was the essence of democratic socialism. In his lifetime that struggle had largely been waged *through*, or in close association with, the trade union movement. In the 1950s and after, there emerged a view among many middle class supporters of the Labour Party that the struggle against privilege had to be redefined as the struggle *against* the privileges of the trade union movement. While Tawney never hesitated to criticise abuses of trade union power and the block vote, he retained to the end of his life the firm conviction that the trade unions and the Labour Party would stand or fall together, and it is in this belief that we must seek the legacy of his socialist commitment.

ANEURIN BEVAN
1897–1960

Kenneth O. Morgan

Aneurin Bevan, incorrigible rebel, prophet and tribune of working class power, appears at first sight an unlikely member of the pantheon of constructive architects of the welfare state. He is often recalled today as a dogmatic irreconcilable. During the thirties he was an implacable critic of the National government. In the war years, he was a remorseless opponent of the wartime consensus and of Churchill in particular.

His years in the Attlee government, from July 1945 to April 1951, were scarred by bitter controversy. To his political opponents, he was a "squalid nuisance," a "Tito from Tonypandy," even "the Minister of Disease." No episode during the Attlee years caused a greater sensation than Bevan's remark, during a speech at Manchester in July 1948, ostensibly delivered to welcome the introduction of the National Health Service, that his Tory opponents were "lower than vermin." The fury of the Tories was, after April 1951, matched by the enmity of his Gaitskellite Labour colleagues. In the fifties, Bevan re-emerged as a party rebel and trouble-maker. The "Keep Left" group and the Bevanite movement became the symbols of savage, internecine conflict within the Labour Party over foreign and defence policy. The formal reconciliation with Gaitskell in the last phase before Bevan's death in 1960 did not greatly alter the picture.

Nothing, indeed, could be more ironic than attempts sometimes made now to contrast the moderate character of the socialism of the Bevanite "legitimate left" with the extremist excesses of Bennery or the Militant Tendency. Aneurin Bevan, in fact, is in danger of passing into prehistory, almost as forgotten a figure as Keir Hardie or George Lansbury in the past. His childhood home in Charles Street, Tredegar, was demolished some years ago with remarkably little public protest.

Yet this stormy petrel was to prove himself, in his five and a half years at the Ministry of Health under Attlee, both a prophet and a great constructive pioneer. He was unusual, almost unique, in the British labour movement in combining a passionate commitment to socialist principles with rare creative gifts of practical statesmanship. He was to prove himself, no less than his fellow-Welshman, Lloyd George, an artist in the uses of power.

Despite all the hammer-blows of financial crises, governmental cutbacks and industrial troubles, the main edifice of the National Health Service still endures as a model of humane social engineering, admired throughout the western world. The NHS alone ought to be proof, if any were needed, that Bevan's contribution to British public life was both positive and creative. The need to propel him out of myth and prehistory into the living world of historical reality is an urgent one. A book on the founders of the British welfare state seems a highly appropriate place at which to begin.

Bevan's appointment by Attlee to the Ministry of Health in July 1945 was something of a surprise. During his earlier career, as MP for Ebbw Vale from 1929, and as a union activist in the South Wales coalfield for years before that, he had not been greatly involved in problems of health and medicine as such. In the thirties, it was unemployment and the means test (later on, Spain and the threat of fascism) that absorbed much of his energy. At the same time, no one could emerge from the crucible of the Welsh mining valleys unaware of how disease, squalor and environmental deprivation enshrouded the lives of the miners and others in the community.

Indeed, a notable aspect of South Wales society from the turn of the century had been the creation of a large array of workmen's health clubs and medical aid societies in the coalfield, often with the aid of Miners' Federation funds through joint subscriptions to hospitals. The private club system worked well; yet it was always bitterly opposed by local general practitioners who resented the element of lay control. In the end, the operations of the National Insurance Act after 1911 killed off many of these private miners' schemes; the conflict between the professional status of the doctors and the social needs of the working class community was already present in microcosm. One of these schemes, a local Medical Aid Society, survived in Tredegar in the 1920s, and the young Aneurin Bevan, along with other young socialists from the Query Club, served on its hospital committee in 1923–24.

Beyond this, Bevan's early involvement with health and welfare seems to have been somewhat indirect. The pressure for a non-contributory national health service to be included in the Labour Party's programme, successfully achieved in 1934, came after all from the professional doctors enrolled in the Socialist Medical Association, men like Somerville Hastings and Stark Murray, rather than from the ranks of union representatives like Bevan at Ebbw Vale.

For all that, it would be wrong to conclude that Bevan emerged at the

Department of Health in 1945 innocent of specialist knowledge of medical matters. The doctors themselves were probably misled by his jovial pronouncement at a medical dinner during his first months in office that "I am a comparative virgin." Medical matters frequently caught the attention of his inquiring and incurably active mind; so did they for his wife, Jennie Lee, herself from a Scottish mining district where similar social deprivation prevailed. Bevan, we know, was much stirred by the Clement Davies committee report on the anti-tuberculosis services in Wales in 1939, which depicted in graphic terms the consequences of damp, insanitary housing, environmental neglect and inadequate public services for lung disease in the valleys. He also had close doctor friends like Dan Davies of Pontycymmer.

More generally, Bevan's concern with the range of socio-economic issues during the thirties provided him with a broad synoptic diagnosis of the interrelated character of employment, welfare, health, education and the other components of a civilised society. They left him with a deep scepticism of the vested interests of middle class groups such as the medical profession. Additionally, from his early days before 1914 when he was stirred by syndicalism and *The Miners' Next Step*, he inherited from South Wales a profound commitment to mass popular involvement and accountability in public services, and to the full panoply of democracy, political and industrial. It was not a bad equipment to bring to bear to the Ministry of Health in the heady days of Labour's electoral victory in 1945.

The National Health Service is invariably recalled as Bevan's major achievement in this period. At the same time, it ought to be noted here that there were other important areas where his role in the creation of the welfare state was crucial and decisive. One was housing. This is often thought to be a blemish in Bevan's record. Slow progress in house building was attacked at the time, while Bevan himself gave hostages to fortune by observing once blithely (and quite wrongly) that he spent a mere five minutes a week on housing during his time at the Ministry of Health.

Certainly, the housing programme of 1945–51 began badly and had several endemic problems. There were endless difficulties of coordinating the housing drive, with responsibility diffused between the Ministries of Health, Supply, Town and Country Planning, and Works, with the Scottish Office having its own responsibility north of the border. There were frequent conflicts for building materials such as bricks, timber and steel between the competing needs of council houses, hospitals, schools and factories in once depressed areas. There was no agreed procedure for ensuring that building starts were kept in line with the availability of labour on a local or regional basis; the list of half-built houses grew steadily.

On the other hand, the crushing problems that Bevan faced ought also to be given due weight. There were ceaseless financial difficulties, culminating in the severe cutback of the local authority housing programme from over 200,000 to 170,000 in 1949. There were constant shortages of raw materials, notably softwood and other timber. There were problems of the allocation of skilled labour, far beyond the control of the Ministry of Health. And there was the legacy of the ravages of the wartime blitz which imposed a huge strain on the resources for urban development. In the circumstances, Bevan's achievement of 1,016,349 permanent houses constructed in the six years to 31 October 1951 (excluding Northern Ireland) comes out impressively enough. Again, given the circumstances of the time, the decision to concentrate on council house building via the local authorities (who controlled sites and planning machinery) for homeless working class families, rather than private housing for sale designed for the middle class, was surely right.

Another area where Bevan was much involved was the social insurance schemes intended to implement the Beveridge proposals. Here the main architect, of course, was another Welsh ex-miner, James Griffiths, Minister of National Insurance from 1945 to 1950, a man as firmly on the Labour right as Bevan was located on the left. In fact, the two men worked well together, and waged a joint campaign on the Labour Party Home Policy Committee in 1948–49 to have the nationalisation of the private assurance companies placed on the party manifesto, to reinforce the legislative achievements in social insurance and health.

In the end, Herbert Morrison and others managed to achieve the watered-down proposal for "mutualisation," a scheme under which ownership would be distributed between policy-holders. This appeared on the nationalisation "shopping list" in the February 1950 election manifesto, but was subsequently buried. Only in the 1970s did Labour again turn to consider bringing the industrial assurance companies, with their huge, untapped investments, within the fabric of a comprehensive public social service.

But it was, of course, the National Health Service that was always Bevan's main preoccupation. Indeed, after the war years, with Beveridge, the Willink scheme of 1944, and several other proposals for revamping the health and hospital service, it was generally anticipated that a new publicly financed health service would be a major priority for the Labour government. And, on this basis, Bevan's initial dealings with the British Medical Association were amiable enough, while his relations throughout with the presidents of the three royal colleges (Surgeons, Physicians and Obstetricians) were even cordial, especially with Lord Moran of the RCP. Like an earlier Welsh politician, Bevan could "charm a bird off a bough" when he tried.

But problems soon began to emerge. Some resulted, perhaps, from the advanced nature of some of Bevan's proposals. In health as in other spheres, it is wrong to make too much of the continuity between the wartime social consensus and the welfare politics of the postwar Labour government. Beveridge had its limits.

Bevan's schemes went notably beyond those of Willink in 1944, especially the latter's final watered-down version. Bevan markedly increased the overall central control of the ministry. He provided more encouragement for new group partnerships in "under-doctored areas" and for local health centres. He was unambiguous that there should be a salaried element in the remuneration of the general practitioners, even though capitation fees would still be the main component of a doctor's salary. Above all, there was a decisive commitment to the national-isation of hospitals, with a comprehensive reorganisation of the hospital governing system under regional boards. This was something of which the Willink scheme, with its tenderness towards smaller and voluntary hospitals, had always fought shy.

The nationalisation of hospitals was the only issue which caused major dispute within the cabinet. On 18 October, and again on 20 December 1945, Herbert Morrison, with his long experience of local government on the London County Council, led the resistance of those who sought to preserve voluntary and municipal hospitals under local rather than national control. Morrison urged that there was no authority in the party manifesto for such a proposal (which was true). He emphasised the role of civic and local pride, and voluntary enthusiasm. He also attacked the proposal to make the cost of the hospitals a full charge on the Treasury (to which Hugh Dalton, the Chancellor of the Exchequer, had already agreed). "There would be a very large transfer of liability from the ratepayer to the taxpayer." Morrison was backed up by the Home Secretary, Chuter Ede. But the great majority of ministers, not only left-wingers like Ellen Wilkinson and Emanuel Shinwell, but more centrist figures like Arthur Greenwood and Tom Williams, strongly backed Bevan up.

An authoritative voice was that of the aged Lord Addison, once Lloyd George's Minister of Health in 1919–21 and himself a notable founder of the welfare state, now Leader of the Lords under Attlee. Addison had himself been an anatomist of immensely high profes-sional reputation; he was also the founder, in effect, of the Medical Research Council. He warmly supported Bevan now on the grounds that a nationalised system would assist the teaching of doctors and the training of nurses. Addison's voice carried much weight with his close friend, Attlee, and the cabinet endorsed Bevan's plans overwhelm-ingly.

But the main reason for the problems that arose lay not in the radicalism of Bevan's proposals – which, when introduced, won the warm support of such notably non-socialist organs as *The Times*, *The Economist* and the *Lancet*. It lay rather in the mulish intransigence of the BMA and its spokesmen, the elderly Dr Guy Dain, chairman of the BMA council, and its serpentine secretary, Dr Charles Hill, who had won fame on the air as "the radio doctor."

The association recognised that Bevan had made many concessions, including the preservation of private practice, pay beds in hospitals (which Bevan himself regarded as detestable but inevitable), the waiving of limits on specialists' fees, and appeal procedures for doctors to NHS tribunals. Nevertheless, it regarded the threat of a full-time salaried service as present, which posed a fundamental menace to the professional freedom and security of the general practitioners. The BMA and its *Journal* also claimed to view the new powers vested in the Ministry of Health, and of the executive councils which would supervise GPs, with alarm. Dr Alfred Cox, absurdly, even denounced Bevan as a "medical Fuehrer."

The outcome was that negotiation between the BMA representatives, largely drawn as they were from wealthier, suburban doctors, and the ministers and his civil servants broke down. Although the act to create the NHS was carried in parliament by a huge majority, the BMA threatened the same campaign of intransigence and obstruction as they had done to another Welshman, Lloyd George, back in 1911. The *British Medical Journal* warned doctors that, like his Celtic predecessor, Bevan was both "a bard and a warrior." The emollient approach of the Welshmen (like that of the Scotsman, Ernest Brown, and the Englishman, Henry Willink, before him) could not be taken on trust.

The period from the summer of 1946 until the final capitulation of the BMA in May–June 1948, and its acceptance of the inevitability of the NHS, is an undistinguished interlude in the history of the British welfare state. Bevan himself struck the wrong note at times. In exasperation, on 9 February 1948 he launched a fierce broadside at the BMA representatives as "a small body of politically poisoned people." He condemned the "squalid political conspiracy" which had led to the terms on medical salaries – now to be much augmented after his acceptance of the Spens report – being so misrepresented. But Bevan had been goaded beyond measure by the extraordinary negativism of the BMA spokesmen, an attitude which the *Lancet* frequently and outspokenly condemned, notably in its issue of 21 December 1946. There were grave doubts (voiced by Henry Souttar, a past president of the BMA) as to whether the views of the ordinary GP were necessarily being fairly represented by the BMA council. Furthermore, there was powerful pressure by Moran and Webb-Johnson, on behalf of the royal specialist colleges, to try to break the professional intransigence of the BMA. Eventually, Bevan ended the impasse by a tactical manoeuvre that made no concession of major substance. While retaining all the central features of the NHS scheme – the nationalisation of hospitals; the regional boards and executive councils; the redistribution of practices; the abolition of the sale of practices – he agreed with Moran's private suggestion that an act might be introduced to affirm that no whole-time salaried service would be introduced by ministerial regulation, and that the fixed element of remuneration of £300 would last only three years and then remain optional only. He confirmed, too, that doctors would have complete freedom to publish their views on the administration of the NHS – not that this had ever seriously been in question. He looked forward to an era of "friendly cooperation."

After that, Dain's diehard obstructionism seemed out of touch, even with grassroots doctors' opinion. A month before the NHS was to be launched, without their waiting for the official advice of the BMA representative body, it was announced that 26 per cent of English practitioners had already joined. Significantly, the proportion was much higher in Wales and Scotland. Shortly after the act came into operation, Bevan announced that 93.1 per cent of the population were enrolled under the NHS. The popularity of the service was henceforth never seriously in doubt. It was Bevan's, perhaps Britain's, finest hour.

Bevan's main preoccupation after that was to ensure that the NHS that he had created would be given adequate funding. As he commented, quite fairly, in his book, *In Place of Fear* (1952), he had given deep thought to the financial basis of the health service, and had strongly resisted any attempt to impose a contributory insurance system here. In fact, the financing of the health service proved to be a recurring problem, and one that somewhat damaged Bevan's reputation as an efficient social service minister.

In 1949, the NHS estimates proved to be inadequate, and supplementary estimates were brought in. Morrison and other ministers complained that economies elsewhere, in capital investment in industry, housing, education and the like, were not being matched by any such sacrifices on behalf of the sacred cow of the health service. With much reluctance, Bevan accepted the principle of a shilling charge on prescriptions on 20 October 1949, but it was understood that there was no immediate likelihood of this being implemented.

In March–April 1950 there was a fierce battle with Sir Stafford Cripps who had succeeded Dalton as Chancellor and who now wished to introduce charges on spectacles and dental services. Bevan told the cabinet on 3 April 1950 that "the abandonment of the principle of a free and comprehensive health service would be a shock to their supporters and a grave disappointment to socialist opinion throughout the world." Aided by Bevan's long friendship with Cripps, going back to Popular Front days, it was agreed to shelve the charges. A ceiling of £392 million was placed on NHS expenditure for 1950–51, and Bevan's own proposal of a cabinet committee (including Addison) to provide a constant review of health finance was accepted.

A year later, the same issue blew up, fuelled by the huge cost of the rearmament programme adopted under American pressure during the Korean war. This time the outcome was disastrous. Cripps had gone; Gaitskell, the new Chancellor, was relatively inexperienced and tactically inflexible, as well as being a target for Bevan's personal rivalry. With Attlee shortly to retire to hospital, and Morrison temporarily in charge, things went from bad to worse. The cabinet committee divided on Gaitskell's proposals on dental and ophthalmic services, and on health appliances. In full cabinet, Bevan was supported only by Harold Wilson and, somewhat mildly, by George Tomlinson. Even Addison now turned against him. The ailing Ernest Bevin's compromise scheme for a £400 million ceiling on expenditure fell by the wayside. Bevan himself, now at the Ministry of Labour and goaded elsewhere by trade union "unofficial" militants, declared that, for the sake of a totally unrealistic defence programme, the government were "departing from Labour Party principle" and from socialist idealism for the sake of a "paltry" £23 million. When Gaitskell's view prevailed, Bevan promptly resigned and internal party bitterness of great intensity ensued for many years.

The whole episode was coloured by partisan and personal issues. In retrospect, Bevan's case looks a powerful one. The £4,700 million defence budget was unrealistic, as the next Conservative government soon confirmed. Churchill himself was to cut it back substantially that December. The health service charges (only £13 million for 1951–52) were a minute item in so vast a budget; Hilary Marquand, Bevan's successor at Health, actually complained on 26 April 1951 that any economy resulting from the new charges would be undermined by the huge and unprecedented rush for dentures and spectacles before the charges would take effect in the summer. Above all, a fundamental principle, bearing on the relation between public health and private means, had been eroded. The theoretical conception underlying one of the great achievements of the British welfare tradition had been weakened with permanent and damaging long-term effects.

Bevan's resignation in April 1951 was the pivotal moment of his career. It should be viewed not so much in terms of protest at the government's foreign policy or rearmament programme, but rather as a rearguard action on behalf of a fabric of comprehensive, single-standard welfare which Bevan himself, along with Griffiths, Addison and others, had largely built up. Beyond the smoke and fury of the controversies of 1951, which seem remote enough now, several points emerge. One is the solidity of the administrative and (for some years) the financial structure of Bevan's health service. The Guillebaud committee of 1956 gave the efficiency of its operations a broad endorsement. So have historians since, though a full examination of the arguments for and against centralism and localism must await Dr Charles Webster's forthcoming authoritative study of the NHS in its early phase.

Another conclusion is the health service's broad reasonableness. A genuine compromise was effected, in 1946 as in 1911, between state direction and professional independence. Generous provision had been made for both general practitioners and consultants within the framework of administration. Indeed, the Socialist Medical Association, with its call for a vast extension of health centres and an end to private medicine, openly voiced in its journal its disappointment at Bevan's relative lack of socialist zeal.

A final verdict must focus on Bevan's rare fusion of the talents of the visionary and of the constructive reformer. He always sought power wherever it resided, even if you "always saw its coat-tails disappearing round the corner." He upheld the "principle of action" which would make socialism practically effective, rather than cherish his doctrinal purity in the wilderness of opposition. In power, as Minister of Health, he exemplified his own generous ideal, that "the emotional concern with individual life is the most significant quality of a civilised human being."

RICHARD TITMUSS
1907–73

Jim Kincaid

A decade after his death in 1973, the work of Richard Titmuss remains a massive presence in the study of the welfare state and in the political debate about its scope and objectives. Those who read his books today are likely to be impressed by the continuing relevance of their themes.

Richard Titmuss is an eloquent defender of Beveridge-style welfare – the large state schemes which aim to provide coverage for all or most of the population. He develops an unrelenting polemic against the sort of welfare policies which returned to dominance in the Conservative Party after 1979 and which proposed the de-nationalisation of broad areas of the current welfare services, the extention of market principles, and a shift towards a more limited pattern of safety net selective provision by the state.

What the reader of Titmuss cannot expect to find is any overall consistency of political or theoretical position. His books contain an extraordinary blend of two different and warring elements. On the one hand, there is a sustained questioning of the proclaimed goals of the social services, and a cool demystification of the values implicit in the actual operation of social policy. Here, for example, is Titmuss – in his *Commitment to Welfare* – on community care for the mentally ill:

"In 1951, eight psychiatric social workers were employed full-time by the 145 local health authorities. In 1959 there were 26, an increase of 2.25 per year . . . In 1959–60 expenditure by local authorities on all mental health and mental deficiency services was approximately £3.5 million. If we allow for price inflation, and for the increase in the total population of the country; for the larger increase in the total of mentally ill people *in the community* seeking or needing treatment (judged by turnover, diagnostic and discharge rates) . . . it is probable that we are spending a smaller amount per head on community care for the mentally ill than we were in 1951. And what we are spending today is substantially less than the sum of £4.9 million paid out in compensation and expenses in dealing with fowl pest in Great Britain in 1959–60."

But there is also another Titmuss. Repeatedly in his work there is an intense celebration of the British welfare state as a living embodiment of altruism and social integration. A secularised version of the Christian socialism of R.H. Tawney, who had a deep influence on Titmuss. A non-marxist alternative to the acquisitive selfishness of the capitalist market.

Titmuss was born in 1907 and was brought up in modest circumstances. His father had worked a small farm in Bedfordshire until he was driven out by the agricultural depression of the 1920s to try his luck in London. An attempt to start a haulage business in Hendon, first with horses and then lorries, proved a failure. He died in 1926, heavily in debt.

Titmuss had left school at 14, and completed the only formal education he was ever to get by taking a six-month course in bookkeeping at the local commercial college. After his father's death Titmuss secured a clerical position in the County Fire Insurance Company. He remained with this firm for 16 years and showed a particular aptitude for the actuarial side of the insurance business. His career flourished, and he achieved the rank of inspector at the unusually early age of 32.

Meanwhile he had married, and it was Kay Titmuss who turned his interests to political questions and supplied him with the drive and confidence to start researching and writing on social statistics. During the 1930s Titmuss lived a double life. In working hours, the insurance office – but in the evenings and at weekends, the actuarial skills learned in insurance work were brought to bear on data about birth rates, poverty and ill-health. By 1938, when he was 31, he had completed and published a book called *Poverty and Population*. Two further books on similar themes appeared within the next five years.

At the time, population questions were at the forefront of domestic political debate. One issue, in particular, was widely and fiercely discussed. In the 1920s and 1930s, throughout most of the industrialised world, birth rates fell sharply, and in Britain by more than in any comparable country. Titmuss shared the common anxiety that this would undermine the imperial role.

"Can we maintain our present attitude in India," he wrote, "while we decline in numbers and increase in average age concurrently? Can we in these circumstances retain our particular status in the world, our genius for colonisation, our love of political freedom and our leadership of the British Commonwealth of Nations?"

This was in a book, *Parents' Revolt*, which he wrote together with Kay Titmuss. In it he demonstrated that the decline in average family size had affected all social classes. He explained this as a mass revolt against the values of an aquisitive economic society based on individual competition and greed: "Capitalism is a biological failure; it is promoting the extinction of society."

The Titmusses also said that there had been a specific revolt by women against "the sacrifice of the best 20 years of their lives to the drudgery of housework." (In the 1970s, their daughter, Ann Oakley, was to publish a series of powerful studies on housework and the sexual division of labour.) They argued for family allowances and for a Keynesian attack on unemployment, but considered that these remedies would still be insufficient. The answer was to create a society of cooperative values that would seem worth bringing children into.

But in Titmuss's early work, and cross-cutting these themes of national efficiency and moral regeneration, there is another theme, equally emphasised, and with a much sharper radical edge. Titmuss is appalled by the scale of wastage of life in Britain. He meticulously calculates the number of lives that would be saved if the working class rates of infant and maternal mortality were as low as those prevailing in the higher social classes. His conclusion is that 90,000 lives each year are being unnecessarily lost.

These early books brought Titmuss a growing reputation and wide contacts among the leaders of liberal concern about social questions – people such as the Cadburys, Seebohm Rowntree and Eleanor Rathbone. In 1942 he was given a full-time appointment in the Cabinet Office to write a history of the work of the wartime Ministry of Health. When this appeared in 1950 as the large volume, *Problems of Social Policy*, it was hailed as a masterpiece.

Ostensibly it is a book of specialist interest only, focusing on three limited areas of wartime social policy – the evacuation of children from the big cities, the improvisation of a national hospital service, and assistance for victims of bombing. In covering these topics, narrative detail and statistical evidence are vividly and elegantly interwoven. But the wider appeal of the book arose from the skilful way Titmuss used these three instances of social policy to construct a broader historical parable. The message was that social unity and high national morale had been achieved during the war because the power of government had been energetically used to provide necessary help to *all* citizens, irrespective of income and social class. Under the pressures of war, two kinds of social divisiveness had been undermined.

First, it had been a principle in prewar social policy that the middle classes should not be eligible for state welfare benefits. Titmuss argued that the exclusion of confident and articulate social groups from welfare encouraged the contemptuous treatment of those dependent on benefits.

Wartime bombing changed this:

"Damage to homes and injuries to persons were not less likely among the rich than the poor and so the medical and financial assistance provided by the government to counter the hazards of war carried little social discrimination and was offered to all groups in the community."

Titmuss argued that such provision on a universalist basis created a new precedent.

But bombing had a further consequence. If the interwar welfare state had been largely reserved for workers, the continuing role of the Poor Law had been to draw a line *within* the working class. Again Titmuss illustrated how the emergencies of war had helped to erode the means test. Attempts by Poor Law officials to means-test the dazed victims of bombing raids had provoked strong public opposition, and had been abandoned at government insistence. Here was a further crucial step in the development of a less discriminatory social policy.

The Beveridge plans, and their postwar implementation, were attempts to generalise these two developments in wartime social policy. There was a state welfare system, universalised by the admission of the middle classes into the schemes. The role of means-testing was reduced by extending the coverage of national insurance, and by the introduction of benefits like the family allowance, which was paid to mothers irrespective of their income.

But Titmuss played no part in this re-organisation of the welfare state. Throughout the 1940s, he was confined by civil service protocol to the role of official historian. It was not until 1950 that he left the civil service and re-emerged as a commentator on current issues of welfare policy. In that year he was appointed to the first chair of social administration at the London School of Economics, one of the very few non-graduates who have ever become professors. He remained in this post until his death, producing a steady flow of books and exercising a growing influence through teaching and reserch. He initiated and developed a style of analysis which was to prove exceptionally powerful and influential. His brilliance lay in the skills of "critical social accounting" – ie, the quantitative assessment of all the various ways in which the power of government is used to distribute and redistribute resources between different categories of the population.

The classic exposition of his approach is an essay called "The social division of welfare." Here he argues that both the defenders and the critics of the postwar welfare system have committed a major error in confining the debate to those sectors of government activity in which services of cash are directly supplied to individuals. Substantial cash benefits are also provided via the tax relief system and to the advantage of the better-off. In addition, large amounts of tax relief are given to support the occupational welfare system. Companies supply favoured categories of their employees with fringe benefits like pensions, sick pay, cars, houses or help with school fees. These are financed with money which otherwise would appear as company profits and be taxed as such.

There are thus two welfare states, and Titmuss is able to show that, in the tax relief sector, the benefits are not only enormous, but heavily concentrated on the higher income groups.

In the 1950s, this was innovative thinking. If it sounds familiar now, this is only because Titmuss and successors like Peter Townsend and Frank Field have persistently continued this type of analysis ever since. It is also because the proportion of national resources allocated via tax relief – "tax expenditure" is the current phrase – has continued to grow yearly.

Titmuss used social accounting mostly to explore the role of government in promoting social class differences in living standards. Others have employed the same techniques to assess racial and sexual inequalities. If a major charge on the taxpayer is financial and medical provision for old people, then the very low proportion of elderly people in the black population means that black taxpayers are subsidising the white population. Again, so long as child care and housework are systematically devalued as sources of welfare entitlement, as compared with employment in the economy, then the state is helping to organise the exploitation of women by men. A further example is international aid. Titmuss calculated that the amount of aid given to the third world by the industrialised countries was worth less than the trained manpower which moved from the third world to work in the west.

As practised by Titmuss, social accounting led to the creation of a new academic discipline. Previously, "social administration" had been an innocuous study of legislative detail thought useful for future social workers, together with an uplifting account of the moral progress of the nation from the inhumanities of Victorian Poor Law to the generosities of Beveridge. Titmuss's influence transformed social administration into an analytic study of social policy, a search for explanations of how and why state power affects the social allocation of every type of financial, welfare and environmental resource.

In other ways, however, Titmuss's record in the post-1950 period is open to serious question. Although an impassioned defender of Beveridge-style universal welfare schemes, he was reluctant to advocate the incorporation of private sector medicine, housing, education and social security into enlarged state schemes which would be truly universal in scope. Such hesitations are strange, because the essential conclusion of his social accounting was to expose the myth that the private sectors are genuinely independent and financially self-sufficient. Public schools are state-aided by being treated as charities for tax purposes. Owner-occupiers and occupational pensions are massively state-subsidised by tax relief. The skilled personnel who staff the private hospitals and the laboratories of the drug companies have been expensively trained by the state. A socialist conclusion would surely be that the large subsidy flows into the private sector of welfare should be used instead to improve standards in the main state schemes for the whole population. This could be most effectively achieved by the nationalisation of the private sectors into an enlarged and reorganised state system.

But though a Labour Party member after 1950, Titmuss remained committed to the Liberal creed of his youth. In the interests of individual freedom, he rejected the demand for drug company nationalisation, and in the case of the pension funds called only for a stricter state supervision of their investment policies. Titmuss remained caught in the classic double-bind of liberal idealism. The coexistence of privilege and poverty is recognised as disgraceful and inefficient. Yet state power can only be sparingly used to attack privilege, because the state is seen as a potentially dangerous enemy of individual freedom, the most cherished value.

In all of his searching analysis of social class inequality, Titmuss almost nowhere discusses inequalities of political and economic power. The single notable exception is a famous essay called "The irresponsible society." Here Titmuss attacks the social power wielded by property companies and pension funds. But in answer he can come up with no kind of democratic alternative. The general political solution he offers is that "those who hold positions of power should set examples for the younger generation in moral leadership and social responsibility."

Here we are at the limits of Titmuss as a radical critic. A serious attempt to nationalise the private welfare system would provoke bitter resistance from the upper middle classes in defence of their subsidised benefits. Such a battle could not be won by a Labour government playing by the normal rules of parliament and Whitehall, but only by a politically mobilised and militant labour movement.

Titmuss recoiled from such a prospect, just as he lined up with the LSE authorities against the student insurgency of the late 1960s. He saw the task of the welfare state as the promotion of social harmony, not the encouragement of class conflict. In his last book, *The Gift Relationship*, he quotes Solzhenitsyn with approval: "What we have to show the world is a society in which all relationships, fundamental principles and laws flow directly from moral ethics and from them *alone*."

It is in this same book that he argues that the British blood donor scheme offers an ideal model of how welfare provision should be organised. The scheme is administered by the state, yet depends entirely on voluntary and altruistic giving. But as a model that could be generalised, this is hopeless. Taken seriously, the argument points to a welfare state run on principles of private philanthropy. To give blood costs nothing beyond a little trouble and discomfort. But the extraction of taxes is a highly painful process, and can hardly be left to individual inclination.

The issue of means-testing in welfare trapped Titmuss into further inconsistencies. He had argued powerfully and repeatedly that means tests could not be run without stigma and social divisiveness, and were highly wasteful to administer. Yet he spent five years as a part-time member of the Supplementary Benefits Commission – the core institution of means-tested welfare.

The contradictions which run through Titmuss's work are certainly not those of intellectual incoherence or indolence. The simple fact was that he had deep roots on *both* sides, in some of the main ideological conflicts of his time. It may not be very consistent to believe that the welfare state is a fine embodiment of British decency, and that real power in Britain is wielded by a greedy and irresponsible ruling class. But both views are widely accepted, and surprisingly often by the same people.

Ultimately, Titmuss's hospitality to divergent views was disabling. His work remained episodic. He could arrive at no clear and articulated political programme. But this very openness, allied to the energy of his research and writing, gives his work a different sort of value. It will continue to be read as a deeply felt record of the political concerns and passionate debates of three decades of British social history.

DRAWING CONCLUSIONS

David Donnison

Sixteen reformers are a very small sample of the people who contributed to the evolution of British social policies over the century and a half spanned by their working lives. Many others might have figured in this book: Thomas Chalmers, the Church of Scotland minister in Glasgow who is often regarded as the founder of modern social work; John Simon, the government's first medical officer of health; Florence Nightingale whose influence extended far beyond the field of nursing for which she is most famous; Charles Loch of the Charity Organisation Society who was on the ultimately losing side in so many of the battles in which the Webbs fought; Neville Chamberlain who was one of our greatest Ministers of Health; Eileen Younghusband who did so much in more recent years to shape the development of social and community work . . . every reader will extend the list in different directions.

Behind them all stand other figures who helped to shape the changing framework of ideas within which the reformers operated: Jeremy Bentham, Karl Marx, John Stuart Mill, Herbert Spencer, Sigmund Freud and Maynard Keynes – some of them briefly glimpsed in this book – were among the most important of them. Then there were the story tellers, dramatists, popularisers and journalists – the great communicators who did so much to change public perceptions and feelings: Charles Dickens, Jack London, W.T. Stead, H.G. Wells, Bernard Shaw, George Orwell, Kingsley Martin and many others. Equally important and more numerous by far were the innovative administrators, local politicians and leaders of public service professions who actually created and managed the "welfare state" and left their imprint upon its ethos and practices. They in turn operated within a framework of pressures and possibilities emanating from society at large and its changing social and political movements.

Nevertheless, provided we place them in this broader context and resist temptations to exaggerate their importance, some speculative conclusions can be drawn from the experience of these sixteen founders of the welfare state. First, what factors and circumstances led to the acceptance or the rejection of their proposals; why did they succeed or fail? Second, what kinds of people were they, and what were their roles within the wider society? Third, what common themes, if any, are to be found in their thinking; do these amount to a distinctive tradition of social policy? I ask these three questions in this concluding essay, in the hope that the answers to them may help us reflect on a fourth and final question. What can today's reforming spirits learn from these pioneers that may help them contribute in some way to the next stage in the development of social policies?

Success and failure

What led to the success or failure of the prescriptions offered by these pioneers? Where very large resources were required – as they were for major new schemes for social security, education, housing, health services and the like – action had to wait on the political flood tides which make such changes possible. Individuals and small groups can neither mobilise such tides nor arrest them.

Much of what was done in the years immediately after 1832, 1905, 1918 and 1945 would have been unthinkable a few years earlier or later. The mobilisation of tax resources for war, followed by opportunities for redeploying them as hostilities cease; the fear stirred up among the ruling classes and the temporary sense of comradeship brought about by threats to the survival of the nation; the slow process of discrediting existing systems and the accumulation of knowledge and ideas within political movements determined to build a better world: all these play a part in the story. The pioneers' influence may then become vital in determining the paths to be taken by the reforming tide.

But every experienced reformer knows that the time for action rarely lasts long. Tides go out again. Thus when the opportunity comes there is scant time for research or experiment, and whatever is done has to be based largely on ideas and experience gathered much earlier, often in very different circumstances. Many of Chadwick's ideas originated with Jeremy Bentham who died in the year when the royal commission inquiring into the Poor Laws – Chadwick's first great project – was set up. Proposals for the decasualisation of labour, formulated by Booth and Beveridge long before the first world war, were put into practice after the second world war. Titmuss's most important policy proposal – the scheme for a wage-related pension scheme which would break out of the Beveridge system of flat rate contributions and benefits – was first published in the mid-fifties. It finally got into the statute book in Barbara Castle's pension scheme 30 years later.

When action is taken, the outcome may be distorted by other influences in ways which distress those who campaigned so long for reform. Josephine Butler, publicly dissociating herself from the prudish campaigns about prostitution mounted after the repeal of the Contagious Diseases Acts, and Ebenezer Howard, whose democratic ideas about new towns were put into practice by development corporations accountable to no one but the central government, were not the only pioneers to suffer this fate.

We must not exaggerate the influence of people who keep diaries, write books and pamphlets, and therefore appear in the histories. Often the most convincing arguments for reform came from the examples set by anonymous innovators working for local authorities. The first workhouses and unions of parishes were set up in the 18th century, long before the Poor Law Amendment Act of 1834. The first experiments in municipal housing began in the 19th century, a generation before the post-1918 legislation which created a national system of local housing authorities. More recently the comprehensive reorganisation of secondary education was modelled on much earlier experiments in Scotland, Anglesey, London and Leicestershire.

These examples should remind us that reform is a continuing process. (Where are the workhouses today?) The new orthodoxy rarely holds unchallenged sway for long. Usually founded on much earlier experience, it soon attracts critics as its defects begin to show. It was Richard Tawney who said: "It is the fate of revolutionaries to supply watchwords to conservatives."

What kinds of people were they?

A first glance suggests that a group more diverse than these pioneers could scarcely have been assembled. But a closer look reveals common characteristics. They were, in widely varying ways, marginal people. Their view of the privileged and the powerful was always sceptical, sometimes angry. Yet they were not "loners"; they belonged to social groups and shared in movements of ideas which – even if they outgrew and discarded them later in life – gave them the conviction and confidence to challenge the dominant establishments of their day.

Edwin Chadwick was the son of a failed businessman who taught him to revere the philosophic radicals and later to work with them; Josephine Butler was born into an Evangelical, radical, professional family, and was taught by her father to study blue books on the social conditions of the time; Joseph Chamberlain was also born into a dissenting tradition as a Birmingham Unitarian; Octavia Hill, granddaughter of a public health reformer, was reared in an impoverished merchant's family; Ebenezer Howard, son of a shopkeeper, emigrated early to America where his main ideas seem to have been formed; Robert Morant was the son of a somewhat impoverished evangelical family . . . and so the tale continues to Richard Titmuss, son of another impoverished, geographically mobile, lower middle class family, who made contact through his spare-time writing with a growing circle of reforming spirits – the Cadburys, Seebohm Rowntree and Eleanor Rathbone, for example. Business failure and illness were familiar in many of the households from which these pioneers came. Perhaps their parents transmitted to them some of their own frustrated determination to make a mark upon the world?

Political leaders have often sprung from the cultural and geographical fringes of the arenas in which they operated. Napoleon, Hitler and Stalin were among the more dramatic examples of a pattern also illustrated, in this respect, by Lloyd George and Aneurin Bevan. But outsiders must become insiders if they are to get a hearing. They must not be *too* marginal.

These pioneers gained acceptance in various ways: partly through the influential radical networks into which some of them were born, or to which they gained access; sometimes through family connections with the aristocracy or the establishment, as in the cases of Josephine Butler and Beatrice Webb; sometimes through local networks of wealth and power, as in the cases of Charles Booth and Eleanor Rathbone in Liverpool, Seebohm Rowntree in York, and Joseph Chamberlain in Birmingham. Radical though their ideas often were, they were presented in ways which could eventually be accepted, at least in part, by powerful groups and movements.

The one common characteristic which helped all these people to gain a hearing was their power to communicate: Joseph Chamberlain, Lloyd George and Aneurin Bevan were among the greatest orators of their generations; Josephine Butler was a vivid public campaigner; the works of Charles Booth, Beatrice (not Sidney) Webb, Richard Tawney and Richard Titmuss are contributions to English literature as well as to research and social reform.

The picture of the social reformer is beginning to take shape: a self-confident, critical outsider, in touch with a supporting network of people and ideas; a highly articulate man or woman, gaining access to the establishment through social, political, academic or administrative networks. But that would still describe a cast of thousands. What distinguishes the real pioneers from the heroes of so many novels who could also be described in this way?

These people had a vision of a better world. That vision was often imprecise in detail – which can be a tactical strength if you have to pick up unforeseen political allies – but the general directions in which it led were clear enough. So were the horrors from which the reformers sought to release us. Some of them were most shocked by oppression, some by poverty, some by inefficiency, some by corruption, and many by a mixture of all these things. It was the politicians among them who attacked injustice in the most comprehensive terms. Joseph Chamberlain asked: "What ransom will property pay for the security it enjoys?" and Lloyd George denounced Britain which, with "more wealth per head of population than in any other land in the world . . . tolerates so much poverty among her people, . . . what is wanted is fairer distribution." Both would be treated today as wildly irresponsible men.

A capacity for rage was common to all these people: Chadwick's against "baleful money interests," political "jobocracies" and "ignorant local administrators"; Josephine Butler's and Eleanor Rathbone's against the oppression and brutalisation of working class women; Octavia Hill's at slum conditions and the human degradation they involved; Tawney's against privilege and all "the vulgar irrelevancies of class and income"; and Titmuss's against the complacent rich who deplored the growth of social services for ordinary people while themselves extracting far more from the state in tax reliefs and in tax-supported benefits from their employers – each of them illustrate this common theme.

Their passion and commitment were motivated by, and expressed in, working lives which led them into many fields of action. None were confined to one profession, one organisation or one social milieu. Particular institutions played crucial parts in these exchanges: in the first half of the 20th century the Fabian Society, the London School of Economics and Toynbee Hall are repeatedly glimpsed in these stories.

Most of these founders of the welfare state were confronted from time to time by the harsh realities of poverty, squalor and injustice. Thus they made links between different fields of social action and different sectors of the economy which were not made by others who knew more about particular specialisms. Beveridge's most famous report, building policies for employment and the health services into a comprehensive plan for social security, was an example of this widely ranging imaginative capacity. The 1909 Minority Report of the Poor Laws Commission, largely written by Sidney Webb, was another. Some of the most radically creative insights into the links between economic, social and psychological aspects of society were to be seen in Josephine Butler's analysis of the situation of women. To this capacity for combined economic and social analysis Ebenezer Howard added further, spatial, dimensions through his grasp of land use and design possibilities.

Effective social reformers are feet-on-the-ground, head-in-the-stars people. Lloyd George at his best was one of the greatest of them. They formulate specific proposals and programmes and are skilled at seizing every opportunity for pushing ahead with them. But they are not mesmerised by institutions. For they know that the most important changes will only be brought about as human beings themselves change. Their proposals are therefore designed to free people from the constraints which cripple and corrupt them. Their short-run opportunism operates within a longer-term strategy – a strategy that is based on a fundamentally optimistic conviction about the capacity of their fellow countrymen to live better lives and to create a better world if only they can be given the opportunity to do so.

Common themes

These generalisations too easily suggest that British social policy evolved smoothly from philosophic radicalism to democratic collectivism as successive pioneers, building on the foundations laid by their predecessors, paved the way for their successors. That impression is reinforced by omitting from this book people (Thomas Chalmers and Charles Loch, for example) regarded in their day as innovative reformers, whose contributions have been submerged or washed into backwaters by the flow of history – or by what we now take to be that flow. What were in their day major institutions of social administration (such as the Evangelical missions, the friendly societies and medical clubs, the churches and their schools) have been omitted from the story, along with the people who created them. Yet similar institutions still play major parts in the social programmes of neighbouring countries.

The evolution of social policies is in reality a confusing process; full of dead ends, conflicts and setbacks. The central motives of the pioneers – Edwin Chadwick's passion for rational efficiency, Josephine Butler's concern for oppressed women, Ebenezer Howard's vision of a healthy human environment made possible by drawing on the enhanced land values which a developing community creates for itself, Richard Tawney's dream of Christian fellowship – were significantly different and do not add up to a consistent philosophy.

To make progress towards those objectives called for the creation or transformation of major institutions and movements involving thousands – sometimes millions – of people, all with motives of their own and with interests to defend. Thus philanthropy fought the growing powers of local government, and local government fought the growth of central government; the resistance of friendly societies to national insurance could only be bought off by asking them to run – and thereby distort – large parts of the system; for two generations the churches' defence of their schools blocked the creation of effective local education authorities; the growth of housing authorities confined housing associations to a backwater; and the resistance of doctors to a national health service could only be overcome by exploiting divisions within the profession. The unspoken function of every successful social pioneer is to blight the hopes and block the pathways of other potential pioneers. In countries not far off similar battles had different outcomes, and significantly different institutions and priorities emerged.

Meanwhile, on the broader scale, the values which these pioneers helped to incorporate in the nation's social conscience were flawed – or so later generations would say – by cross-cutting ideologies. Imperialism was one of these. Joseph Chamberlain's populist demands for social justice did not extend to the Irish. As a result he played a leading part in splitting the political party which was the nation's principal vehicle for social reform. Octavia Hill's proposals for housing reform were crippled by her hostility to the state which had eventually to become the principal instrument for demolishing the slums and rehousing the poor. Beveridge's assumptions about the family and the role of women within it seem, with hindsight, to have built major defects into the system he helped to re-fashion. There is nothing surprising about this. Successful pioneers have to share enough of their fellow citizens' prejudices to gain their support for reform.

Nevertheless, although there is a shortage of clear-cut common principles in the evolution of British social policies, common tendencies emerge in action, often as a by-product rather than a major objective of the reformers' campaigns. I shall reflect briefly on two of these tendencies: first about equality, and then about the role of the state.

Equality was rarely an objective in its own right for these founders of the welfare state. Tawney, Bevan and Titmuss came closest to presenting an explicitly egalitarian philosophy. But even Tawney, whose book, *Equality*, is still well worth reading, was primarily concerned with fraternity – a sense of community. But "What a community requires . . ." he said, "is a common culture, because, without it, it is not a community at all. . . . But a common culture cannot be created merely by desiring it. It rests upon economic foundations. . . . It involves a large measure of economic equality."

For others the typical starting points for campaigns which ultimately were to lead in equalising directions were a sense of shock at the squalor, pain and poverty they saw around them, and a rejection of their predecessors' inadequate responses to these problems. The stumbling story of the slow growth of public understanding of these issues is briefly glimpsed here and there in this book.

Chadwick's attack on relief given in aid of wages prompted him to distinguish paupers from the working population and to offer them minimal support which would compel them to fend more effectively for themselves. Booth's demonstration that such a regime was irrelevant to the large proportion of the poor who were beyond working age led to his proposals for old age pensions. Rowntree's research, which showed that the poor were not a separate, submerged tenth but a much larger proportion of working class people who fell into poverty at three predictable stages of their lives, led him to call for nationwide policies which would provide assured minimum standards of living for all. The Webbs pointed out that the state would have to intervene in depressed times to ensure that sufficient jobs were available for those capable of working, and called for the break-up of the growing array of local services provided specially for the poor, and their replacement by nationwide services available to the whole population. Eleanor Rathbone pursued the implications of these arguments for family support. Beveridge, starting from studies of the labour market, was led to propose labour exchanges, and later a whole system of insurance benefits, family allowances and health services which would provide much of the national minimum called for by Rowntree. Lloyd George and Bevan played their crucial parts in implementing many of these proposals. But Titmuss demonstrated that new forms of exclusion and impoverishment constantly emerge in a fundamentally unequal society, and that the state is implicated in this process in all sorts of ways, providing tax reliefs and encouraging employers to provide tax-supported occupational benefits which are among the most unequal features of our society. The rich, not only the poor, and all the major institutions of society, not only its social services, will have to be on the agenda of policy makers who are really determined to eliminate the evils associated with poverty.

Few of the founders could be described as egalitarians on principle. As practical people all of them recognised the enormous variety of human capacities and preferences. But the gradual evolution of their understanding which I have so briefly sketched led them and their followers to advocate policies which had increasingly egalitarian implications. That was where a basic capacity for outrage about human suffering, coupled with a growing understanding of the complex task of putting things right, was ultimately bound to lead.

The second set of trends which flowed from these debates was likewise an implication of the reformers' arguments rather than their main objective. The politicians and those social analysts who got involved in political action were repeatedly led to enlarge the powers of government – and particularly those of the central government. They encouraged the development of a functional, service-orientated style of administration, and strengthened the increasingly specialised professions which manned these public services. Institutions like the London School of Economics and Political Science (founded by the Webbs, directed by Beveridge, with Tawney and Titmuss on its staff and most of the other figures in this book on its reading lists) educated many of the people who entered these public services as administrators, economists, social workers, teachers, town planners and so on.

Chadwick was most brutally clear about the enemy to be defeated: "ignorant local administrators" and "the sinister interests which operate most powerfully in narrow areas." Looking at the losers rather than the winners, we can see these trends unfolding in the successive defeats of the untrained, the amateur and the local – the local Poor Law, local philanthropies, local friendly societies. The winners were more professional, more centralised, more uniform and more expensive.

Underlying these trends were other assumptions which gradually became increasingly deeply embedded in the culture of the period: the assumption that in time the wealth of the nation and the resources for public services would grow, and that this would enable governments to help the poor without reducing the living standards of the average citizen; the assumption that across a broad range of opinion – in the Labour and Conservative parties, in the civil service, the liberal professions and the media – more and more people would in time come to share similar concerns about poverty and adopt similar egalitarian philosophies; the assumption that power holders would eventually be led to support these developments by social research and analysis; the assumption that the public service professions could generally be trusted to work efficiently and humanely; and hence the assumption that the evolution of social policies could be planned by social scientists and put into practice by "social" ministries. Meanwhile economic development could be left to "economic" ministries and the economists.

The founder figures themselves would often have rejected these crude ideas. But their more sophisticated views were widely misunderstood and over-simplified – which is why a man like Ebenezer Howard, who was centrally concerned with the social potentialities of economic development, was redefined in public mythology as a physical planner who designed new towns.

The future

All these assumptions about social policy have in recent years collapsed. That was made brutally clear in 1979 by a minister in the newly elected Conservative government, Reg Prentice (himself a former Labour minister).

He explained that if you are convinced that the only way to solve the country's problems is to offer greater rewards for success, that means making the rich richer. And if the national income is static or falling, that can only be done by making the poor poorer.

It was at least an honest statement, demolishing in one breath the assumption that the economy and its public services would go on growing; the assumption that power holders were genuinely concerned about the poor and might be induced to consider ways of giving them a fairer share of the rewards which a wealthy society offers; and the assumption that researchers and social analysts who have expectations of this kind can make a significant contribution to the work of government.

In the following years many more widely held aims and expectations were abandoned: the expectation that maintaining, or getting back to, very high levels of employment would be at the top of every government's priorities; the hope that a growing system of universal benefits would lift more and more people off means tests; and the belief that major social commitments entered into by previous governments, Labour and Conservative alike, would be honoured (the commitment to provide additional insurance benefits in return for earnings-related contributions, and the commitment to provide a university education for students qualified according to the "Robbins principle," for example).

What lessons can we learn from the experience of the pioneers discussed in this book that will help us to respond to these events and make a constructive contribution to the future development of social policies? Reactionary periods of this sort have occurred before: most recently, on a mild scale, in the 1950s, when a number of wartime and postwar advances in social policy were threatened or abandoned; and on a more frightening scale in the thirties, when unemployment pay was reduced, public services were severely cut back, hunger marchers were tramping the land and fascists seized power in many countries. As W.G. Runciman points out, these periods of reaction tend to coincide with economic depression. Reaction tends to be reinforced by victorious small-scale wars (like the Falklands), fought by professional soldiers.

But bad times for social reformers can also be good times for them to reappraise their ideas and to formulate new policies. The most important ideas contributed by those discussed in this book were usually generated, long before they became publicly accepted, in periods when the pioneers were excluded from influence and largely unknown. That is still true today. The ideas of the monetarist economists Milton Friedman and F.A. Hayek, much quoted by

Conservatives after 1979, were developed a generation ago when their authors played no part in the corridors of power.

If this is a time for new thinking, what should reformers be thinking about? They should focus particularly on the two main trends in the evolution of British social policies: the egalitarian stance, and the growth of the state. This is not the place to deploy fresh arguments on these themes, but the experience of these founders of the welfare state suggests some of the directions in which the arguments may lead.

The equalising aims of British social policy were rarely explicit. The pioneer reformers were mainly concerned about other problems – hardship, squalor, human degradation – and their egalitarianism usually emerged as an implication of the solutions proposed for these problems, not as their main objective. More recent pioneers, like Brian Abel-Smith, Peter Townsend and the leading spirits in the Child Poverty Action Group, have since taken a more explicitly egalitarian line. They have adopted a relative view of poverty which is no longer regarded as failure to attain the kind of subsistence minimum advocated by Rowntree and Beveridge but as exclusion from the continually evolving living standards of the average citizen. They have often been described as "rediscovering" poverty, but they were in fact redefining it.

They did not, however, explain to the average citizen why he should adopt this radically new approach to a wide range of social issues. As a result, he still thinks of poverty in Booth's and Rowntree's terms as a matter of subsistence standards or as a problem for pensioners and other vulnerable groups. Some of them still think of it in Chadwick's terms as a matter of destitution and moral failure. It took half a century of research, practical experiment and political mobilisation to get Seebohm Rowntree's new approach to poverty, first published in 1901, publicly accepted and built into social legislation. It may take as long to gain public acceptance for the much more radical egalitarian view now emerging.

The analysis of this issue can no longer be evaded because the philosophers (like John Rawls) are getting their teeth into it, and some of them (like Robert Nozick) reject the egalitarian view root and branch. Their approach is rather legalistic and wholly unhistorical. What social contract would induce free people to join forces and subordinate their individual interests to those of a wider society? What principles for the distribution of the good things of life would they regard as fair, and what powers would they concede to the state governing such a society? These are the kinds of questions from which the philosophers' analysis typically begins.

But a study of the reformers briefly sketched in this book shows that social issues do not in fact present themselves in this way. There was never a state of nature in which free spirits joined forces to make a social contract. Reformers started from a sense of outrage about human conditions, and a rejection of already existing forms of collective action which failed to remedy those conditions. Before the national insurance scheme there were the locally administered Poor Laws, and before them there was charity – just as there were private armies, private fire brigades and private police forces before the state took a hand in providing these things. The questions to be asked are, first, about the nature and origins of social problems. Does poverty matter? In what sense? Why has it been redefined as inequality?

I believe we shall find that poverty, even in the old-fashioned sense of hardship, cannot be eliminated unless we consider the whole economic and social structure and the human relationships characteristic of this structure. Who, then, should take action about these problems? We must ask whether the state — as it is now, or as reformers envisage it might become – is the best instrument for changing these things. Is it more humane, effective and accountable – is it less oppressive – than alternative forms of collective action potentially available? Too many reformers have assumed that the answer to these questions must be Yes.

Titmuss, the last in the line of pioneers discussed in this book, was already more sharply aware than his predecessors that critical questions had to be asked about the state and the public service professions through which it operates. Tawney thought that rapacious business-men could be civilised if only they adopted proper professional codes of conduct. Titmuss was always alert to the possibility that public services, set up to relieve various forms of poverty, might end up reinforcing, institutionalising and justifying the exclusions and humiliations which lie at the core of poverty. Ivan Illich, in his indictment of "disabling professions," later went much further.

Meanwhile other people in many different quarters have been asking increasingly critical questions about the state and the centrally controlled, professionally dominated, service-oriented style of government we have created. A nation whose principal experience of the state is gained from encounters with tax collectors, social security and housing officials, refuse collectors and telephone operators is not convinced that public services are necessarily humane, efficient and accountable to their customers. Although they offer different responses to these more critical views of the state, the Liberal Party's commitment to "community politics," the attempts being made by Labour councils to decentralise services and make them more account-able to local people, the growth of aggressive styles of community and welfare rights work, the demands for stronger democratic control of the police made by the civil liberties lobby, and the Conservative Party's drive to privatise state services and subject them to the disciplines of the market – all these initiatives are addressed, at least in part, to similar problems.

Closely related to these themes are other new developments. The collapse of British industry has compelled people to recognise that the economy on which our incomes and the public services depend, cannot safely be left to develop unaided. Still less can it be left to economists and the central economic ministries. Thus civic leaders are endeavouring to promote the development of their own cities and regions by supporting local enterprises, setting up enterprise boards, promoting community businesses, using housing and other public services to generate demands for locally producible services, and so on. Again the solutions vary, ranging from central government projects such as enterprise zones and urban development corporations to cooperative development agencies and community businesses set up with the help of local councils; but they are addressed to similar problems.

A sharper ear for what the earlier reformers were saying might have focused attention on these issues sooner: Josephine Butler, for example, said "that one of the greatest questions of the future will be that of ascertaining the best means of effectually counteracting or holding in check the strongly bureaucratic tendencies which we see to be stealing over almost every civilised nation." She criticised the "manipulation of the poor, the criminal, scholars in school, etcetera," and called for the "infusion of Home elements into . . . hospitals, schools . . ., asylums . . . and even prisons. . . . Everything lives and thrives best where there is the principle of play or freedom which home affords." And Ebenezer Howard's linked concerns for economic development and local collective action, supported by varied, locally accountable public services, are as relevant today as they ever were.

Turning from future policies to the people who will play leading parts in formulating them, past experience again offers us some guidance. The crucial contributions are likely to be made by people who stand outside the big bureaucracies, the academic and professional establishments and the political parties – people who retain an independent and critical point of view. But these people will also belong to intellectually active groups which offer them stimulation and support. They will retain the capacity to be shocked by poverty and injustice, and get out into the field to meet these problems at first hand. They will probably move easily between the professions and public services, the academic world, the pressure groups and politicians. And they will be capable of communicating vividly and effectively. There will also be pioneers who try out new ways of doing things at local level and show that saner arrangements can be made to work successfully: theirs is a crucial role. No one can do all these things. Hence movements and focal centres linking such people have to be created – successors to (or a rebirth of) the Fabian Society, Toynbee Hall and the London School of Economics.

But innovative ideas and experiments do not by themselves change the world. The opportunity to do that waits on much larger movements. It was the labour movement which provided the essential driving force for so many of the changes traced in the latter part of this book. This movement, based on the more skilled manual workers and the organisations they created – the unions, the Co-ops, the chapels and working men's clubs – is now widely believed to be declining; and it is true that as the older industries decay there are fewer and fewer people of the sort that made up this movement. The millions of unemployed or intermittently employed youngsters who follow them have no fire in which to forge their sense of class consciousness, their collective conviction that the world could be different and their determination to make it so.

But social conflicts and the social changes which eventually flow from them arise from social divisions and the contending interests involved in them. While Britain remains a profoundly unequal society – and it is now growing more unequal – such conflicts are bound eventually to re-emerge in some form. Whether the tides of change they bring with them will flow in humane and healing directions or whether they lead to brutality will depend in part on the quality and relevance of the ideas, the practical experience and the proposals for action generated during the coming years by a new generation of reformers.

NOTES ON CONTRIBUTORS AND FURTHER READING

Preface
PAUL BARKER is the Editor of New Society.

Towards the Welfare State
ASA BRIGGS – Lord Briggs of Lewes – is   Provost of Worcester College, Oxford, and Chancellor of the Open University. His books include *Victorian People, Victorian Cities* and *A Social History of England*.

Edwin Chadwick
RUDOLF KLEIN is Professor of Social Policy, University of Bath, and Joint Editor of *The Political Quarterly*.
Further reading:
S.E. Finer, *Life and Times of Sir Edwin Chadwick* (Methuen, 1952)
R.A. Lewis, *Edwin Chadwick and the Public Health Movement* (Longman, 1952)
M.W. Flynn (ed), *Report on the Sanitary Condition of the Labouring Population of Great Britain by Edwin Chadwick* (Edinburgh University Press, 1965)
S.G. and E.O.A. Checkland (eds), *The Poor Law Report of 1834* (Penguin, 1974)
Lord Robbins, *The Theory of Economic Policy in English Classical Political Economy* (Macmillan, 1978)
Anthony Brundage, *The Making of the New Poor Law* (Hutchinson, 1978)
David Roberts, *Victorian Origins of the British Welfare State* (Yale University Press, 1960)
Sir John Simon, *English Sanitary Institutions* (Cassell, 1890)
Raymond G. Cowherd, *Political Economists and the English Poor Law* (Ohio University Press, 1977)

Josephine Butler
PAT THANE is Senior Lecturer in Social History, Goldsmiths' College, London.
Further reading:
Judith Walkowitz, *Prostitution and Victorian Society* (Cambridge University Press, 1980)
Frank Prochaska, *Women and Philanthropy in 19th Century England* (Oxford University Press, 1980)
A.S.G. Butler, *Portrait of Josephine Butler* (Faber, 1954)
Josephine E. Butler (ed), *Woman's Work and Woman's Culture* (Macmillan, 1869)

Joseph Chamberlain

DENIS JUDD is Head of History, Polytechnic of North London.

Further reading:

Peter Fraser, *Joseph Chamberlain* (Cassell, 1966)

J.L. Garvin, *The Life of Joseph Chamberlain* (vols 1–3) and J. Amery (vols 4–6) (Macmillan, 1932–69)

R. Jay, *Joseph Chamberlain* (Oxford University Press, 1981)

Denis Judd, *Radical Joe: a life of Joseph Chamberlain* (Hamish Hamilton, 1977)

Bernard Semmel, *Imperialism and Social Reform* (Allen & Unwin, 1967)

Alan Sykes, *Tariff Reform in British Politics, 1903–13* (Oxford: The Clarendon Press, 1979)

Octavia Hill

PETER MALPASS is Senior Lecturer in Social Policy, Bristol Polytechnic.

Further reading:

M. Brion and A. Tinker, *Women in Housing* (Housing Centre Trust, 1980)

E. Moberly Bell, *Octavia Hill* (Constable, 1942)

W. Thomson Hill, *Octavia Hill* (Hutchinson, 1956)

E. Gauldie, *Cruel Habitations* (Allen & Unwin, 1974)

D. Owen, *English Philanthropy* (Oxford University Press, 1965)

Charles Booth

PHILIP WALLER is Fellow and Tutor in Modern History, Merton College, Oxford.

Further reading:

T.S. and M.B. Simey, *Charles Booth, Social Scientist* (Oxford University Press, 1960)

Beatrice Webb, *My Apprenticeship* (Longman, 1926); *Our Partnership* (LSE and Cambridge University Press, 1948 and 1975)

Ebenezer Howard

PETER HALL is Professor of Geography, University of Reading.

Further reading:

Ebenezer Howard, *Garden Cities of To-morrow*, with Lewis Mumford introduction (Faber, 1946; reprinted 1965)

Frederic Osborn and Arnold Whittick, *The New Town Story* (Leonard Hill, 1969)

Gordon Cherry, *The Evolution of British Town Planning* (Leonard Hill, 1974)

Walter Creese, *The Search for Environment* (Yale University Press, 1966)

Michael Hughes (ed), *The Letters of Lewis Mumford and F.J. Osborn* (Adams & Dart, 1971)

Martin J. Wiener, *English Culture and the Decline of the Industrial Spirit* (Cambridge University Press, 1981)

The Webbs

JOSE HARRIS is a Fellow of St Catherine's College, Oxford.

Further reading:

S. and B. Webb, *Industrial Democracy* (Longman, 1897); *The Break-Up of the Poor Law* (Longman, 1909); *The Public Organisation of the Labour Market* (Longman, 1909)

Beatrice Webb, *Our Partnership* (LSE and Cambridge University Press, 1948 and 1975)

Norman and Jeanne Mackenzie (eds), *The Letters of Sidney and Beatrice Webb* (Cambridge University Press, 1978); *The Diary of Beatrice Webb* (vol 1) (LSE and Virago, 1982)

R.L. Morant
HARRY JUDGE is Director of the Department of Educational Studies, Oxford University.
Further reading:
B.M. Allen, *Sir Robert Morant* (Macmillan, 1934)
Olive Banks, *Parity and Prestige in English Secondary Education* (Routledge & Kegan Paul, 1953)
E.J.R. Eaglesham, *The Foundations of 20th Century Education in England* (Routledge & Kegan Paul, 1967)
S. Webb, *The Education Muddle and the Way Out* (Fabian Society, 1901)

Lloyd George
JOHN GRIGG is the author of *The Young Lloyd George* and *Lloyd George: the People's Champion,* the first two volumes in a planned five-volume life of Lloyd George.
Further reading:
W.J. Braithwaite, *Lloyd George's Ambulance Wagon* (Methuen, 1957)
H.V. Emy, *Liberals, Radicals and Social Politics, 1892–1914* (Cambridge University Press, 1973)
Bentley G. Gilbert, *The Evolution of National Insurance in Great Britain* (Michael Joseph, 1966)
L.B. Masterman, *C.F.G. Masterman: a biography* (Frank Cass, 1968)
Bruce K. Murray, *The People's Budget, 1909–10* (Ploughman Press, 1980)

Seebohm Rowntree
JOHN VEIT WILSON is Head of the School of Applied Social Science, Newcastle-upon-Tyne Polytechnic.
Further reading:
Asa Briggs, *Social Thought and Social Action: a study of the work of Seebohm Rowntree* (Longman, 1961)
B.S. Rowntree, *Poverty: a study of town life* (Macmillan, 1901); *The Human Needs of Labour* (Longman, 1937); *Poverty and Progress: a second social survey of York* (Longman, 1941)
B.S. Rowntree and May Kendall, *How the Labourer Lives: a study of the rural labour problem* (Nelson, 1913)

Eleanor Rathbone
JANE LEWIS is a Lecturer in Social Administration, London School of Economics.
Further reading:
Hilary Land, "The family wage" (*Feminist Review*, No.6, 1980)
Jane Lewis, *The Politics of Motherhood* (Croom Helm, 1980)
J. Macnicol, *The Movement for Family Allowances* (Heinemann, 1980)
E. Rathbone, *The Disinherited Family* (Edward Arnold, 1924)
Mary Stocks, *Eleanor Rathbone* (Gollancz, 1949)

William Beveridge
TONY LYNES is the author of the *Penguin Guide to Supplementary Benefits.*
Further reading:
Jose Harris, *William Beveridge: a biography* (Oxford University Press, 1977)
W.H. Beveridge, *Power and Influence* (Hodder & Stoughton, 1953); *Social Insurance and Allied Services* – the Beveridge report (HMSO, Cmnd 6404, 1942)

R.H. Tawney

J.M. WINTER is a Fellow of Pembroke College, Cambridge.
Further reading:
R.H. Tawney's Commonplace Book (Cambridge University Press, 1972)
R.H. Tawney, *The Acquisitive Society* (Bell, 1921); *Religion and the Rise of Capitalism* (John Murray, 1928); *Equality* (Allen & Unwin, 1931); *The Attack and Other Papers* (Allen & Unwin, 1953); *The Radical Tradition* (Allen & Unwin, 1964); *History and Society* (Routledge & Kegan Paul, 1978)
R. Terrill, *R.H. Tawney and His Times* (Harvard University Press, 1973)
J.M. Winter, *Socialism and the Challenge of War* (Routledge & Kegan Paul, 1974)

Aneurin Bevan

KENNETH O. MORGAN is a Fellow of The Queen's College, Oxford.
Further reading:
Brian Abel-Smith, *The Hospitals, 1800–1948* (Heinemann, 1964)
Harry Eckstein, *The English Health Service: its origins, structure and achievements* (Harvard University Press, 1959)
Michael Foot, *Aneurin Bevan* (2 vols) (MacGibbon & Kee, 1962; Davis Poynter, 1973)
Almont Lindsay, *Socialised Medicine in England and Wales* (Oxford University Press, 1962)
Kenneth and Jane Morgan, *Portrait of a Progressive* (Oxford University Press, 1980)
J. Stirling Ross, *The National Health Service in Great Britain* (Oxford University Press, 1952)
Richard Titmuss, *Essays on the Welfare State* (Allen & Unwin, 1958)
Kenneth O. Morgan, *Labour in Power, 1945–1951* (Oxford University Press, 1984)

Richard Titmuss

JIM KINCAID is a Senior Lecturer in Social Policy, University of Bradford.
Further reading:
Richard Titmuss, *Problems of Social Policy* (HMSO, 1950); *Essays on the Welfare State* (Allen & Unwin, 2nd edn, 1963); *Commitment to Welfare* (Allen & Unwin, 1968)
D.A. Reissman, *Richard Titmuss* (Heinemann, 1977)
Hilary Rose, "Re-reading Titmuss: the sexual division of labour" (*Journal of Social Policy*, vol 10, No.4, 1981)
Paul Wilding, "Richard Titmuss and social welfare" (*Social and Economic Administration*, vol 10, No.3, 1976)

Drawing conclusions

DAVID DONNISON is Professor of Town and Regional Planning, University of Glasgow. He was previously Chairman of the Supplementary Benefits Commission.
Further reading:
R.H. Tawney, *Equality* (Allen & Unwin, 1931)
W.G. Runciman, *Relative Deprivation and Social Justice* (Routledge & Kegan Paul, 1966)
Peter Townsend, *Poverty in the United Kingdom* (Penguin, 1979)
B.S. Rowntree, *Poverty: a study of town life* (Macmillan, 1901)
John Rawls, *A Theory of Justice* (Oxford University Press, 1972)
Robert Nozick, *Anarchy, State and Utopia* (Blackwell, 1968)
Ivan Illich, *Disabling Professions* (Marion Boyars, 1977)
David Donnison, *The Politics of Poverty* (Martin Robertson, 1982)

The suggestions for further reading have, in each case, been supplied by the authors.